Collins

CAMBRIDGE
Checkpoint English

Lucy Birchenough, Clare Constant, Naomi Hursthouse, Ian Kirby, Nikki Smith

Series Editors: Julia Burchell and Mike Gould

Stage 7: Teacher's Guide

William Collins' dream of knowledge for all began with the publication of his first book in 1819. A self-educated mill worker, he not only enriched millions of lives, but also founded a flourishing publishing house. Today, staying true to this spirit, Collins books are packed with inspiration, innovation and practical expertise. They place you at the centre of a world of possibility and give you exactly what you need to explore it.

HarperCollins Publishers Ltd
The News Building
1 London Bridge Street
London SE1 9GF

First edition 2016

10 9 8 7 6 5 4 3 2 1

© HarperCollins*Publishers* Limited 2016

ISBN 978-0-00-814053-3

Collins® is a registered trademark of HarperCollins*Publishers* Limited

www.collins.co.uk

A catalogue record for this book is available from the British Library.

Printed and bound by CPI Group (UK) Ltd, Croydon, CR0 4YY

We are grateful to the following for permission to reproduce copyright material:

An extract from *Boy: Tales of Childhood* by Roald Dahl, published by Jonathan Cape Ltd and Penguin Books Ltd, pp.28, 86, copyright © Roald Dahl, 1984. Reproduced by permission of David Higham Associates Ltd and Farrar, Straus, and Giroux, LLC. All rights reserved; An extract from "Look into the eyes of a caged tiger and you will see the zombie victim of 'zoochosis'" by Damien Aspinall, *The Mail on Sunday*, 30/07/2008, copyright © Solo Syndication, 2008; An extract from *Penguin Beach* and *Gorilla Kingdom*, Zoological Society of London, www.zsl.org. Reproduced with permission of ZSL; An extract from 'Endangered species' by Margaret Mittlebach, KIDS DISCOVER Spotlight, www.kidsdiscover.com. Reproduced with permission; An extract from 'Why Zoos Matter', Saint Louis Zoo, www.stlzoo.org, copyright © Saint Louis Zoo. Reproduced with permission; An extract from *Game of Thrones: Book One of A Song Of Ice and Fire* by George R. R. Martin, Harper Voyager, pp.7–9, copyright © George R. R. Martin 1996. Reproduced by permission of HarperCollins Publishers Ltd and Bantam Books, an imprint of Random House, a division of Random House LLC. All rights reserved; An extract adapted from *Eragon* by Christopher Paolini, published by Corgi Children's, pp.6, 10. Reproduced by permission of The Random House Group and Penguin Random House LLC; Extracts from *Elidor* by Alan Garner, pp.30–32, copyright © Alan Garner, 1965. Reproduced by permission of HarperCollins Publishers Ltd and Curtis Brown Group Ltd, London; An extract from *Jimmy Coates: Revenge* by Joe Craig, pp.117–118, 236–237, copyright © Joe Craig, 2007. Reproduced by permission of HarperCollins Publishers Ltd; and the poem 'The Magic Seeds' by James Reeves published in *Complete Poems for Children*, Faber Finds, 2009, p.118, copyright © The Estate of James Reeves. Reproduced by permission of Artist's Estate via Laura Cecil Literary Agency.

If any copyright holders have been omitted, please contact the publisher who will make the necessary arrangements at the first opportunity.

This text has not been through the Cambridge endorsement process.

Series Editors: Julia Burchell and Mike Gould
Commissioning Editor: Ben Pettitt
Development Editor: Lucy Hobbs
Managing Editor: Sarah Thomas
Project Manager: Maheswari PonSaravanan at Jouve
Copy Editor: Sonya Newland
Proofreader: Ros Davies
Typesetter: Jouve India Private Ltd
Cover design: Lucy Harvey at ink-tank and associates ltd

Contents

Chapter 6 • Writing to analyse and compare

Chapter 7 • Testing your skills

Worksheets

Blank Check your progress sheets

Introduction

Welcome to the Collins Checkpoint English Teacher Guide 1. We hope it will provide useful support to teachers worldwide, as they prepare students for the freedom, challenge and enrichment offered by the Cambridge Secondary 1 course for Stage 7.

Using the Student Book

The Student Book is structured so that it builds the fundamental skills that underpin success at the end of Stage 7. It is divided into seven chapters. Each of the first six chapters focuses on a different writing 'purpose', while the seventh offers the chance to put all the skills into practice through exam-style tasks.

Chapters 1 to 6 address these different purposes in detail and cover the Stage 7 learning objectives that relate to them:

* Writing to explore and reflect

* Writing to inform and explain

* Writing to argue and persuade

* Descriptive writing

* Narrative writing

* Writing to analyse and compare

Chapter 6 focuses on literary analysis. While this is not a requirement of the Cambridge Secondary 1 English curriculum framework or assessments, it nevertheless has the benefit of both broadening the range of material students encounter and beginning to embed skills at a basic level, which will be useful in literature studies.

Chapter 7 offers a series of resources for assessment practice. While these can be used separately to secure a particular assessment style, as each question type is covered, they could also be set together as a more formal 'mock' end-of-stage assessment.

Features of the Student Book

Each of the first six chapters is based loosely on a theme such as 'good deeds' or 'mystery and suspense' and enables students to learn and practise a range of general reading, writing, speaking and listening skills, in particular those that are part of writing for the featured purpose. Students will read a wide variety of texts from writers from many social, cultural and historical backgrounds and will write a wide range of texts themselves. Each chapter provides them with opportunities to complete two substantial tasks to show what they have achieved: one on reading and responding to texts, and one on writing for each type or purpose. From these, you will be able to assess students' work to see how their abilities are developing across the learning objectives for Stage 7.

The book has also been designed so that students revisit particularly important skills several times across the chapters. In some cases, this is to make sure that they can apply the skills in new contexts; in others it will be because a new aspect of the skill has been introduced to help them to progress. Key features of the book include Check your progress panels at the end of each two- or four-page unit. These will help students to assess their own progress. Three other text features to note are Checklist for success panels, which list criteria that students should cover when completing a task; Key terms panels, which define important literary and language terms; and Vocabulary panels to support students when reading an extract.

Using the Teacher Guide

Each two-page (or four-page) section in the Student Book is intended to provide work for one lesson (occasionally two), and is supported in the Teacher Guide by a one- or two-page lesson plan, plus worksheet(s) and PowerPoint slides (PPTs).

The Teacher Guide is designed to help you with the following.

Planning

- Key references to the specification for Stage 7 are listed at the start of each lesson plan, with the **learning objectives** identified so that the wider application of learning is clear.

- Detailed, ready-to-use **lesson plans** offer all you need to teach. These are divided into sections that match the Student Book – *Introducing the skills*, *Developing the skills* and *Applying the skills* – ensuring progression and pace in the activities, as well as opportunities for consolidation of the learning.

- **Worksheets** and **PowerPoint slides** (PPTs) supplement and extend activities in the Student Book. These are itemised in each lesson plan, meaning that time-consuming preparation is kept to a minimum.

Differentiation

- Each lesson plan begins with **learning outcomes** differentiated by level of achievement so that you can monitor the level at which students are working and help them progress.

- Further differentiation opportunities are provided in the **Give extra support** and **Give extra challenge** boxes, ensuring that all students are stimulated towards reaching their potential.

- **Worksheets** and **PPTs** offer additional activities and support mechanisms to suit a range of learning styles and abilities.

Assessment

- Chapter 7 revisits the assessment questions from the Student Book, offering additional guidance on how to help students self-assess their work.

- Peer- and self-assessment are regularly used to help students understand how to progress towards their target level of achievement. Any success criteria included in the book are our own.

Our resources are designed to enhance performance so that candidates can work towards the next stage of the Cambridge Secondary 1 course with confidence. We hope you enjoy using them.

Julia Burchell
Series Editor

1.1 What is writing to explore and reflect?

Learning objectives
7Rv2

Checkpoint progress test
• Paper 1, Section A

Differentiated learning outcomes
• **Lower: All students must** identify different types of personal writing.
• **Mid: Most students should** highlight the key purpose of different pieces of personal writing.
• **High: Some students could** adapt the style of their writing according to the type of personal text.

Resources
• **Student Book**: pp. 8–9
• **Worksheet**: 1.1
• **PPT**: 1.1
• **Workbook links**: Unit 1.1, pp. 5–6

Introducing the skills

Students should work alone to read the introductory sections on page 8, describing the different types of personal writing. To prepare for Question 1, ask them to draw up a list of biographies and autobiographies that they know of. These can be about sporting legends, movie stars and pop celebrities, politicians or people who have led remarkable lives in different ways. Can students think of any books that have been published in the form of diaries or journals?

Give extra challenge by asking students to make suggestions about why each person from the biographies/autobiographies they have listed has had their personal 'story' told in this way.

Developing the skills

Look at Question 2. Discuss with students how the people listed had a specific reason for writing their autobiography or for being written about. Ask students to make a separate list of all the people that they would *like* to read about in a biography or autobiography, giving reasons for their choices.

Reinforce the difference between narrative (thoughts and feelings) and non-narrative (facts and statistics) information to prepare for Question 3. Students should use Worksheet 1.1 to develop their ideas linked to this question and writing about a specific event.

Applying the skills

Before students write the full paragraph for Question 4, they could practise thinking about and writing in all four different styles. Show them the slides in PowerPoint 1.1 as a summary reminder, and then ask them to create starter sentences for the table on slide 3. This will help them decide which form to use for their full paragraph.

Give extra support by referring back to Question 1 in the Student Book to remind students of examples of starter sentences.

Plenary	At the end of the task, get students to swap books to read each other's completed paragraphs. They should try and identify the type of personal text it is by the way it has been written.

Cambridge Checkpoint English
Stage 7

Learning objectives
7Rx1; 7Rx2

Checkpoint progress test
• Paper 1, Section A

Differentiated learning outcomes

• **Lower: All students must** skim a whole story to work out the writer's 'big idea'.

• **Mid: Most students should** find key words in a starter sentence that give clues about the 'big idea'.

• **High: Some students could** scan a story to find 'small points' that link to the 'big idea'.

Resources

• **Student Book**: pp. 10–13

• **Worksheet**: 1.2

• **PPT**: 1.2

• **Workbook links**: Unit 1.2, pp. 7–8

Introducing the skills

Remind students that when writing about an event, place or person, writers choose to focus on different things. Their choice is usually linked to the overall message (the 'big idea'). They may exclude other information if it does not correspond to this point of view. For example, if someone is writing about a ruthless tyrant, they may choose to exclude the fact that this person was kind to their own children.

Ask students to write ten pieces of information about themselves in a bullet-point list. They should then swap their lists with a partner, who should write *one* sentence summarising the writer based on the information in the list. For example:

This person is very adventurous and particularly likes playing sport.

Are students surprised at the conclusions their partners have drawn based on the information they provided?

Give extra challenge by asking some students to write three additional pieces of information about their partner that give a *different* impression of them from the one they summarised based on the original list.

Show students slide 1 of PowerPoint 1.2 to remind them of the key terms for this topic. They could copy these into their books to refer to as needed.

Students should then read the description of Mrs Pratchett on page 10 of the Student Book and complete Questions 1 and 2. Go through the correct answers as a class, taking time to discuss why the statements are true or false according to the information provided by the writer.

When students have completed Question 3, talk together about the different pieces of information ('small points') they have chosen that helped them decide on the writer's point of view. Use slide 2 to show students how they can scan for words in the text that help describe the writer's point of view, using the example given ('loathsome'). Remember, scanning is used to find specific information in a text. In this instance, students are not looking for a particular word, they are looking for *describing* words linked to the idea of the character being 'loathsome'. This means that all the words they find should contain some description linked to the big idea that the writer does not like Mrs Pratchett. Students should check the words they have chosen against slide 3.

Developing the skills

Before students complete Question 4, remind them that the purpose of a starter sentence is to give the reader a clue about the content of a story before they start reading it.

The starter sentence in Question 5 suggests that the text will be about the writer's experience of being poor. Before moving on to Question 6, ask students to write down all the things they associate with being poor. Then, as they skim the text they will more easily pick out relevant information based on the clues in the starter sentence. Remind them that skimming is quickly moving your eyes over a text to get a general understanding of its content without reading every single word.

> **Give extra support** by providing key categories for students to link with the idea of being poor, such as 'clothes', 'home', 'food'.

Once they have completed Questions 7 and 8, students should use Worksheet 1.2 to consider in more depth how descriptive words are used to link to a big idea. To match the words to the starter sentences, they will need to work out what big idea the writer is going to present in the rest of the story.

> **Give extra challenge** by asking students to choose one of the starter sentences from Worksheet 1.2, and then carry on the paragraph, using appropriate words for the big idea.

Applying the skills

Discuss students' thoughts on the big idea and small points in Questions 9 and 10. Notes like this can be used as preparation for an extended piece of writing. Display the sample student paragraphs on slide 4, which have been written using small points. Using their own small points, students should work in pairs to decide which paragraph gives the most accurate representation of the extract and why.

Feed back to the class, explaining that the first response has understood the general idea that the boarding school seems like a harsh place that the writer is unlikely to enjoy. However, it makes assumptions about the writer's feelings, such as that he 'misses home'. This is not mentioned in the text.

> **Give extra support** by directing students to link the comments made in the sample responses with relevant points in the text.
>
> **Give extra challenge** by asking students to change or add any comments of their own that they think would improve either of the responses.

Plenary	Use slide 5 to check students' learning about how to extract information from texts.
	Read the statements aloud one by one. Students should go to one of four corners of the room (marked with each of the titles as indicated) or write their answer on a mini-whiteboard or piece of paper to hold up. Alternatively, they could put their hand up when you call out the one that corresponds to their idea.
	Note that the answers are not necessarily exactly right or wrong. There is opportunity here for discussion about each one, especially in cases where students have given different responses to one another.

<table>
<tr><td>

Learning objectives

7R01; 7Ri1; 7Rw1

</td><td>

Checkpoint progress test

- Paper 1, Section A

</td></tr>
</table>

<table>
<tr><td>

Differentiated learning outcomes

- **Lower: All students must** use inference and deduction to work out meaning.
- **Mid: Most students should** identify similes and metaphors in writing.
- **High: Some students could** make an informed personal response, explaining the use of implicit and explicit meaning.

</td><td>

Resources

- **Student Book**: pp. 14–17
- **Worksheet**: 1.3
- **PPT**: 1.3
- **Workbook links**: Unit 1.3, p. 9–10

</td></tr>
</table>

Introducing the skills

Before students answer Question 1, remind them that factual details are *explicit* – they do not require readers to work out anything for themselves using inference or deduction. Talk through the definition of these terms using the 'Key terms' panel on page 14 of the Student Book to ensure students fully understand the tasks they will be doing in this topic.

Ask students to write a list of emotions (sadness, anger, etc.). They should then create five explicit statements using some of these emotions. Get students to write in the first person. For example:

I was angry when my sister dropped my phone.

Ask students to swap their books. Using the five explicit statements their partner has written, students should try to *deduce* something about that person's character. Remind them that deduction is adding up all the information in a text to find an overall meaning. So, a series of statements about getting worried, anxious or upset might lead someone to deduce that their partner is quite stressed.

Explain that writers often convey a lot of emotion in their work, but it is not always explicit. Recap the difference between explicit and implicit meaning in writing using slide 1 in PowerPoint 1.3. As a class, work through the examples on slide 2 to decide what emotion the red words are *implicitly* suggesting.

Students should then read Jackie Kay's description of her father and complete Questions 2–4, looking for explicit and implicit meaning.

Give extra challenge by showing students the different sentence stems on slide 3, including the example given in the Student Book, to allow them to develop their thoughts and explanations of the meaning in the writing.

When students have finished these questions, ask them to complete Worksheet 1.3 to consolidate their understanding of the skills practised so far.

As a homework task or quiet writing task at the end of a lesson, students could write a description of themselves using both the explicit and implicit sentences on appearance and emotion that they have created.

Developing the skills

Once students have completed Questions 5 and 6, get them to reinforce their understanding of similes and metaphors by doing one or more of the following activities.

1. Choose one of the similes or metaphors in Question 5 and use it to write one paragraph of a story that includes further similes and/or metaphors. Students could then swap their work with a partner and identify these techniques in their partner's writing.

2 Take each of the statements in Question 5 and change them from similes to metaphors or vice versa.

3 Write five similes and/or metaphors about their own lives, their family, their school etc.

Applying the skills

In order to successfully analyse writers' use of language and give an informed personal response to a piece of writing, students need to look at individual words as well as how they relate to one another. To help with this, spend some time reviewing the text in this section before students answer Question 7. Focus on individual words and how they connect to build an overall picture. For example, in the phrase *nightmare of endless vehicles*:

- The word 'nightmare' suggests that the situation is so bad that it seems unreal, like a dream. Nightmares are often also quite frightening, which implies that this situation is quite alarming for those experiencing it.
- The word 'endless' suggests that the situation is carrying on and on, and implies that this is both boring and frustrating.
- Putting the two words together gives a sense that although you can usually wake up from a nightmare, the scary part of this situation is that there seems to be no end. The writer is eternally trapped behind a great number of other vehicles in the same predicament.

Students may find the sentence stems on slide 3 useful when completing Question 7.

Give extra support by working with students in small groups as they talk through their ideas and plan their responses to Question 7. Listen to their discussions and offer guidance where appropriate.

Plenary

It is important that students understand how to check their own work and peer-assess each other's. Once they have completed Question 7, tell students swap books with a partner. Show them slide 4 and ask them to use the list to check each other's work. They could write the numbers 1 to 6 at the bottom of the piece and mark each number with a tick or cross to indicate whether it includes the stated evidence.

When they have completed the assessment, help students write comments for their partner to help them improve their writing. They should give a comment, focusing on the point of learning. Encourage students to avoid comments such as 'well done' or 'very good', which do not offer advice. They should identify areas of strength and make 'target' suggestions on what could be done to improve the writing.

Students should then swap back and spend 10 minutes revising their writing according to the recommendations given by their partner.

Responding to personal writing

Learning objectives

7R01; 7Ri1; 7Rw1

Checkpoint progress test

• Paper 1, Section A

Differentiated learning outcomes

• **Lower: All students must** write their own paragraphs about the text using the starter sentences provided.

• **Mid: Most students should** complete the reading paper practice test.

• **High: Some students could** reflect on their areas of strength and need for improvement.

Resources

• **Student Book**: pp. 18–21

• **Worksheet**: 1.4a & 1.4b

• **PPT**: 1.4

• **Workbook links**: Unit 1.4, pp. 11–12

Your task

Briefly recap the reading skills covered in Topics 1.1, 1.2 and 1.3. Explain to students that they need to write two paragraphs about the extract based on two of the skills they have investigated so far:

• the big idea and the small point that reveal this
• the writer's thoughts and feelings and how they identify them.

To consolidate and check their understanding of the learning in this chapter so far, give students Worksheet 1.4a and ask them to draw lines match the key terms on the left with the definitions on the right. Afterwards, discuss any areas where students are uncertain.

Briefly explain the setting for the extract from *Cider with Rosie*.

Give extra support by reading the text aloud to students before they start the task. Hearing the imagery read in an adult voice will help shape their understanding of the overall meaning.

Approaching the task

Before students begin to analyse the text, it may be helpful to check their knowledge of all the vocabulary it includes so that this does not interfere with their overall understanding. Ask them to point out any words they do not recognise and spend five minutes looking them up in the dictionary.

Discuss the text as a class. A conversation around what is happening in it will ensure that students have a general understanding of the content before they approach the specific elements of the activities. They should then complete Questions 1–4 on their own.

Question 3 asks students to find and explain implicit meanings in the text. If students need more support for this activity, display slide 1 of PowerPoint 1.4, which provides options from which they can choose the five they understand best to analyse in their answer.

Either before or after students write their two paragraphs for Question 5, help them investigate the text further by giving them the sample exam questions on Worksheet 1.4b. Afterwards, display slides 2–4 on PowerPoint 1.4 and talk through the answers with students, unpicking why they may have gone wrong if they have made mistakes.

Finally, ask them to create two bullet-point lists. One to detail the big idea and small points they will cover in paragraph 1 and the other to detail the feelings they will cover in paragraph 2. They should then complete Question 5.

Reflecting on your progress

Questions 6 and 7 can be completed before or after you have assessed students' responses to Question 5. If completed before, then students can present and label a 'before' and 'after' answer (i.e. their original answer and an improved version) so that the progress made in response to these activities can be seen.

Note that if you are teaching these tasks before assessment, students will only improve aspects of their response that they can identify as in need of improvement. In this case, it may be useful to read through the two responses with the annotations and comments, and then ask students to identify similar areas in their response and to annotate these before making improvements. You could also emphasise that evaluating a student's current level is of secondary importance to the progress they can make during this session, and that this will be rewarded by the teacher afterwards.

If these tasks are to be completed *after* teacher assessment, then students can draw on the teacher's assessment comments to identify where improvements need to be made, as well as the example responses, annotations and comments.

Afterwards, students can work in pairs, using slide 5 as a guide to peer-assessing and validating the improvements made. The writer should point out the deficiencies that they recognised in their first attempt and how they improved them. Alternatively, students could be asked to work independently to annotate their improved responses by identifying and labelling the changes they made with an explanation of why what they have done is an improvement.

Plenary 	Students have already spent some time checking their work in this chapter. Display slide 6 and ask students to use the skills sentences to write a summary of their assessment on their own writing.

Controlling language in a presentation

Learning objectives
7SL1; 7SL2; 7SL4; 7SL9

Differentiated learning outcomes
- **Lower: All students must** write a short anecdote about themselves for presentation.
- **Mid: Most students should** use language to make their presentation interesting for the audience.
- **High: Some students could** vary the delivery of the presentation to keep the audience engaged.

Resources
- **Student Book**: pp. 22–23
- **Worksheet**: 1.5
- **PPT**: 1.5
- **Workbook links**: Unit 1.5, p. 13

Introducing the skills

Explain to students that an effective presentation needs two things – good content (what is being said) and good delivery (how it is being said). If good content is poorly delivered, a presentation will not be successful.

When students have answered Questions 1 and 2, show them slide 1 in PowerPoint 1.5 to help consolidate their ideas. Ask students to write two headings – 'What' and 'How' – and put the words on the slide under the correct heading. Review the answers on slide 2 together.

Before students complete Question 3, get them to think about different ways of delivering a speech by showing them slide 3. Perform the task as a class, with everyone standing up. Go down the bullet list repeating the phrase 'Go and see the head teacher' in all the different ways described. Discuss the effect of the different styles of delivery.

Developing the skills

Put students in pairs or small groups and ask them to talk about books they have read whose beginnings and endings they find particularly memorable. Why do they think this is? Students should then complete Question 4 on their own.

Applying the skills

Worksheet 1.5 offers students practice in creating a semantic field. Get them to carry out these activities before doing Questions 5 and 6. When creating the semantic field for their own presentation, show them slide 4 of PowerPoint 1.5 and encourage them to list their words in the appropriate column.

Give extra support by asking students to annotate their speeches with notes on where they wish to deliver it in specific ways, such as with emphasis, hand gestures, increasing pace.

Give extra challenge by asking students to use a thesaurus to change five of the words in their lists to a word they do not usually use. Make them think about how changing a word changes the meaning of a sentence ever so slightly – does it still say what they want it to?

Plenary To consolidate learning in this topic, show the class slide 5. Get them to work together to put the statements in order from the most to the least effective type of presentation.

Using verb tenses for effect in writing

Learning objectives
7Wp4; 7Wp5

Checkpoint progress test
- Paper 1, Section B

Differentiated learning outcomes
- **Lower: All students must** distinguish between different forms of the past tense.
- **Mid: Most students should** be able to convert verbs into the past tense.
- **High: Some students could** write about the past using different forms of the past tense.

Resources
- **Student Book**: pp. 24–25
- **Worksheet**: 1.6
- **PPT**: 1.6
- **Workbook links**: Unit 1.6, pp. 14–15

Introducing the skills

Elicit from students as many verb tenses as they can think of. Depending on their general language skills, this may be as simple as past, present and future, or they may know of other forms. Discuss the purpose of each tense and decide on definitions for them – for example 'past' = something that happened before now.

When students have completed Questions 1 and 2, ask them to do the tasks on Worksheet 1.6. This could be an independent or homework exercise to consolidate the skills from this section and prepare for Questions 3 and 4.

Developing the skills

Use slide 1 in PowerPoint 1.6 to review the different verb forms. Explain (or ask students to explain) what each form means in terms of its placement in the past (e.g. past = a completed action). Remind students of what we mean by a 'verb phrase'.

Move on to slide 2. Either work through the paragraphs as a class, choosing the correct phrases, or get students to work in pairs to write out the paragraph with the correct verb forms. Students then complete Questions 3 and 4.

Applying the skills

Students should complete Question 5 on their own. Help them if necessary by providing the following starters:

- When I woke up this morning…
- As I was walking to school…
- My first lesson today was maths…

Give extra support by reminding students of the auxiliary verbs 'be' and 'have'. Instruct them to use the words 'was' and 'had' twice each in their writing, as this will guide them to use verb phrases of the past continuous and past perfect.

Give extra challenge by asking students who complete Question 4 or 5 quickly to rewrite either the text provided or their own paragraph completely in the present tense.

Plenary

Students should swap books to check each other's work. They are looking for two examples of each of the past tense forms. They should give each other a mark out of six for finding these.

Cambridge Checkpoint English
Stage 7

1.7 | Using vocabulary precisely in personal writing

Learning objectives

7W02; 7Wa7

Checkpoint progress test

- Paper 1, Section B

Differentiated learning outcomes

- **Lower: All students must** add detail in writing with adjectives and adverbs.
- **Mid: Most students should** use adjectives and adverbs to determine the specific meaning of writing.
- **High: Some students could** choose synonyms to vary detail and meaning.

Resources

- **Student Book**: pp. 26–27
- **Worksheet**: 1.7
- **PPT**: 1.7
- **Workbook links**: Unit 1.7, p. 16

Introducing the skills

Use PowerPoint 1.7 slides 1 and 2 to enhance students' understanding of adjectives and adverbs. They should fully understand the type of words that each describes and how effective adjectives and adverbs are in adding detail, creating images and changing the meaning of sentences.

Use slides 3 and 4 to show students how grouping adjectives in twos or threes helps to build a more effective image for the reader. However, remind them that using more than three adjectives starts to make the image less effective.

Students should then complete Questions 1–4 on their own. When they have done so, they could compare their answers with a partner.

Give extra support by getting students to carry out the activities on Worksheet 1.7 to consolidate their understanding of adjectives and adverbs.

Developing the skills

Remind students that it is easy to over-use some words in writing. 'Nice' is an example of this. Refer them to the word bank, and then ask them to complete Question 5.

Develop Question 6 by asking students to create pairs of sentences with the synonyms they find in the thesaurus. They should write one sentence using the original word from the word bank. Then they should write a second sentence in which the word is replaced with one of their synonyms in the same sentence if it makes sense. If it does not, their second sentence should use the synonym correctly in a different context.

Applying the skills

Ask students to complete Question 7 on their own. They could then share their paragraphs with the class and have a vote on the most effective description.

Give extra challenge by asking stronger students to use *all* the synonyms they have found for one word effectively in sentences. This will challenge them to think carefully about the slight differences in meaning that synonyms can have.

Plenary Use the remaining PowerPoint slides as flashcards, asking students either to write down or call out the definitions of the term or the term for the definition.

Cambridge Checkpoint English
Stage 7

Linking and structuring ideas

Learning objectives
7Wp1; 7Wp6

Checkpoint progress test
- Paper 1, Section B

Differentiated learning outcomes
- **Lower: All students must** identify the subject and verb in a simple sentence.
- **Mid: Most students should** use connectives to make compound sentences.
- **High: Some students could** use a variety of sentences to make their writing flow better.

Resources
- **Student Book**: pp. 28–29
- **Worksheet**: 1.8
- **PPT**: 1.8
- **Workbook links**: Unit 1.8, p. 17

Introducing the skills

Once students have completed Question 1, show them slide 1 on PowerPoint 1.8 and ask them to identify which of the six word types each word is.

Before students do Question 2, talk through slide 2 to reinforce the learning about subjects and verbs in simple sentences. Then ask students to identify the subject and verb in each sentence on slide 3.

Give extra challenge by asking students to create their own sentences with a subject and verb using the following prompt words: *cheese, laughing, superman, pickled onions*. For example, *The cat likes cheese*. (*the cat* = subject; *likes* = verb)

Developing the skills

Remind students that a compound sentence is two simple sentences joined with a connective. Review the grid on page 28 of the Student Book and go through the purpose of each connective with students. Ask them to work in pairs to come up with a sentence using each connective.

Give extra support by displaying slide 4, which shows compound sentences with the wrong connectives. Help students identify the correct connectives for the sentences to make sense.

Applying the skills

Ask students to complete Question 5 on their own. When they have done so, give them Worksheet 1.8 and ask them to complete the assessment activities.

To develop their learning, ask students to write a paragraph about a special day – a festival, their birthday or something they did at the weekend. It should include:

- three nouns and three adjectives
- two proper nouns
- three verbs and three adverbs
- three simple sentences and three compound sentences.

Plenary	Ask students to write one simple sentence and one compound sentence describing what they have learned or done in the lesson. They should underline the verb in each sentence, put a circle round the connective in the compound sentence and put a star next to any describing words they have used.

Cambridge Checkpoint English
Stage 7

Learning objectives
7Wa6

Checkpoint progress test
- Paper 1, Section B

Differentiated learning outcomes
- **Lower: All students must** write a journal entry about a recent event.
- **Mid: Most students should** write their journal entry using appropriate adjectives and adverbs and a variety of sentences.
- **High: Some students could** include implicit and explicit details in their writing, as well as a variety of sentences and different forms of the past tense.

Resources
- **Student Book**: pp. 30–31
- **Worksheet**: 1.9
- **PPT**: 1.9
- **Workbook links**: Unit 1.9, pp.18–19

Approaching the task

Recap with students what information they should identify when reading task instructions – for example, the required form, content, purpose and audience. Once they are clear on these, they could spend a few minutes in pairs noting the implications of those prescribed in the task by making a checklist of features to include. This could then form part of a whole-class collaboration to draw up a checklist, which can be displayed while students attempt the task. They should them complete Questions 1–3 on their own.

Reflecting on your progress

This section of the topic could be used before students write their own piece to help them gain a thorough understanding of how they will be assessed and how to improve their writing. They can use the response examples as models for assessing their own work and can refer back to previous topics to consolidate their understanding as necessary. They can peer-check each other's evaluations before writing the improved versions. Afterwards, you can check both 'before' and 'after' versions to monitor their understanding and progress.

Alternatively, this section can be used after they have written and assessed their journal entries. You can then help them focus on the learning through the most relevant example, response and comments, as well as your own assessment of their work. After completing Questions 4 and 5, students can produce an improved version of their own article to self-assess before awarding themselves an improved level based on the 'Check your progress' points on page 32 of the Student Book.

Give extra support by giving students Worksheet 1.9 to help them identify the various points on which they will be assessed. Slide 1 in PowerPoint 1.9 contains the answers.

Give extra challenge by asking students to work in pairs using progress points 4c–7c on page 32 of the Student Book to annotate each other's journal entries, commenting on where effective skills have been used and suggesting improvements.

Plenary Ask students to review the 'Checklist for success' on slide 2 and choose one main area they have identified as being in need of improvement. They should rewrite that section of their journal entry focusing specifically on the skill in question.

What is informative writing?

Learning objectives
7Rw8; 7Rv4; 7Wa4

Checkpoint progress test
- Paper 1, Section A

Differentiated learning outcomes
- **Lower: All students must** recognise that information texts share common layout features.
- **Mid: Most students should** recognise that information texts may have different features that enable them to suit their purpose.
- **High: Some students could** recognise the specific features of an online news report and make simple comments about how the writer uses these features to suit the text's purpose.

Resources
- **Student Book**: pp. 34–35
- **Worksheet**: 2.1
- **PPT**: 2.1
- **Workbook links**: Unit 2.1, p. 20

Introducing the skills

Students can work in pairs to share examples of information texts. They can also predict which features they think most information texts have, before examining the first article as part of Question 1. This will help reveal students' knowledge of the layout and feature vocabulary.

Developing the skills

Discuss the purpose of online news texts with students (i.e. to engage as well as to inform). Then, when students identify the layout and organisational features in Questions 2 and 3, emphasise the purposefulness of the writer's choices.

Display PowerPoint 2.1 and talk through its content as additional support and preparation for students developing their responses to Questions 3 and 4.

Give extra support by asking students to complete the features of the second article on Worksheet 2.1 as part of Question 2. They should then use the Worksheet to reinforce Questions 3 and 4, identifying features common to information texts and those specific to online news texts.

Give extra challenge by providing students with a different type of information text (such as an information leaflet or an encyclopedia entry) and asking them to annotate the purposes of its layout and presentation features.

Applying the skills

After students attempt Questions 5 and 6, they can peer-assess each other's work. All students could be asked to learn the spellings of the key features.

Plenary

To correct or reinforce their learning, students can play a game in which the teacher calls out a layout or presentation feature. Students stand up if they think the feature appears in most information texts and remain seated if it is specific to online news texts. Additionally, students can be asked to suggest ways in which the feature can support the purpose of an information text, for example, 'How can a heading help make an information text engaging for readers?'

Cambridge Checkpoint English
Stage 7

Learning objectives
7Rx1; 7Rx2; 7Rv4

Checkpoint progress test
• Paper 1, Section A

Differentiated learning outcomes

• **Lower: All students must** use clues to find information in a text.

• **Mid: Most students should** use the features of information texts to find details.

• **High: Some students could** scan a text to find information efficiently and sum up its content.

Resources

• **Student Book**: pp. 36–37

• **Worksheet**: 2.2

• **PPT**: 2.2

• **Workbook links**: Unit 2.2, p. 21

Introducing the skills

Students could work independently to write the labels for Question 1 (if learning the spelling of these features was set as a task last lesson, this is also an opportunity to test their knowledge). Before moving on, unsuccessful students can be taught any terms they need to learn. Successful students could work in pairs to discuss the purpose of each feature as it is used in the text to reinforce the learning in Question 2.

Use PowerPoint 2.2 to help students understand when to deploy different types of reading skills. Then model how to use their knowledge of organisational features to scan and identify the main information in a text.

Developing the skills

Make sure students understand that as well as using a text's features to locate where information is likely to be, they can also scan prose to find a particular word or detail. See if students can find the word 'macchiato' more quickly than 'Starbucks' or '378'. Then introduce the learning about how to use features such as capital letters, figures, etc. to search efficiently.

Give extra support by using the table on Worksheet 2.2 to complete Question 3.

Give extra challenge by asking students to write their own 'search for' questions for a text such as a newspaper article or a web page. The questions should rely on a feature such as numbers, punctuation or fonts. Students could then try to answer each other's questions.

Applying the skills

If students can recall the information asked for in Question 3 without scanning, then encourage them to discuss the most efficient way to find and check the information asked for in Question 4 – for example, find the standfirst because it will have a summary of the story, or scan for the key phrase and read those sentences.

Plenary	Ask students to suggest real-life situations in which scanning is a useful skill. They could also suggest other features that might help them identify different types of information – for example, reading the conclusion to find out the latest information in a news story.

Learning objectives
7Rw5; 7Rv4

Checkpoint progress test
• Paper 1, Section A

Differentiated learning outcomes

• **Lower: All students must** recognise ways in which a text suits its audience or purpose.

• **Mid: Most students should** recognise formal and informal English in a text and ways in which a text suits its audience and purpose.

• **High: Some students could** suggest reasons why the writer's choice of text feature or language suits the audience and purpose.

Resources

• **Student Book**: pp. 38–41

• **Worksheet**: 2.3

• **PPT**: 2.3

• **Workbook links**: Unit 2.3, pp. 22–23

Introducing the skills

Display slide 1 of PowerPoint 2.3 to check students' understanding of the terms 'audience' and 'purpose'. Then display slide 2, which gives examples of different audiences and purposes. Students can work in teams who take it in turns to suggest the different types of text that would suit these audiences and purposes. The other teams have to support or challenge the suggestions, giving their reasons for doing so.

Read Text A on page 38 of the Student Book with students. Model how to consider what type of text you are reading and its content. Demonstrate how these reveal the text's audience and purpose because the text has been specially crafted to suit them. Students should then read Texts B and C, and attempt Question 1 in pairs. Afterwards, ask students to explain which clues in each text helped them decide its audience and purpose.

Remind students that writers craft their texts carefully so that each feature suits the audience they are targeting and achieve the text's purpose. Then ask students to work in groups to discuss Questions 2–4, before feeding back their answers to the class.

Give extra challenge by asking students what changes they would make to Text A so that it would suit young supporters of the campaign, instead of adult officials such as charity trustees. You could provide students with a copy of the text and ask them to annotate it with their ideas.

Developing the skills

Make sure students understand the difference between official and unofficial audiences and purposes for a text. They should be able to identify situations in which it might be appropriate for a writer to use formal or informal English. To support this, you could provide students with an example of an information text produced by your school or college, such as a letter informing parents about a trip, and identify features of formal English within it. Students should then complete Questions 5 and 6.

Give extra support by providing Worksheet 2.3 to help students complete Question 5. This will allow them to spend the task time on the learning rather than losing time constructing their grids.

When students have completed this section, ask them what each type of expressive punctuation listed in the grid can be used to convey. Use this to draw on their experience of reading informal English in text messages, on websites, in instant messaging services, etc. to consider what effects informal English has. Suggestions might be:

- convey emotion
- create tone
- suggest attitude
- create humour.

Ask students to consider whether there would be any advantages for a) reference books and b) legal documents, such as witness statements used in court cases, to be written in informal English rather than only ever in formal English, as is traditionally the case. Students may find this challenging, so carry out this activity as a whole class and give guidance where necessary.

Applying the skills

Students should re-examine Text B for Questions 7–9 and recognise the purposefulness of the contrasting use of informal English used to convey Judith's voice and personal experience in an engaging way. They should also note the more formal English used to make the reader feel confident that the information provided in the report is accurate and believable.

Plenary	Display the phrases 'Informal English', 'Formal English' in the middle of the board and ask students to work in pairs. They have up to one minute to agree on a list of five differences they might notice between texts written in informal and formal English. The first pair to stand up and be able to correctly list five differences are the winners.
	Next, join student pairs into groups. Write the following words on the board randomly positioned around 'Informal English' and 'Formal English':
	<ul><li>reliable</li><li>traditional</li><li>personal</li><li>impersonal</li><li>official</li><li>unofficial</li></ul>
	Challenge students to note down the words and to decide what associations there are between the ideas these words represent. Each concept should have at least two connections to other ideas. These can be represented by drawing lines linking the words to each other in a kind of word web.
	If there is time, students should share their connections and discuss the ideas these represent with the class.

Learning objectives

7Rw5; 7Rv4

Checkpoint progress test

- Paper 1, Section A

Differentiated learning outcomes

- **Lower: All students must** use some of the skills learned when responding to an information text.
- **Mid: Most students should** use many of the skills learned when responding to an information text and make some improvements to their responses.
- **High: Some students could** combine the reading skills they have learned when responding to an information text, and demonstrate understanding of what makes a high-level response to informative writing, including making improvements if necessary.

Resources

- **Student Book**: pp. 42–45
- **Worksheet**: 2.4
- **PPT**: 2.4
- **Workbook links**: Unit 2.4, pp. 24–25

Your task

Briefly recap the reading skills covered in Topics 2.1, 2.2 and 2.3. You could do this by asking students to work in pairs to prepare 30-second briefings. The presentation of these could be enlivened by giving students the extra challenge of presenting their briefing in the style of a well-known personality.

Display slide 1 of PowerPoint 2.4, which contains the task for this topic. Ask students to identify information about the **form** the writer should use, what kind of **content** to include and the **audience** and **purpose** the writer needs to suit. Then display slide 2 and challenge students to decide whether each piece of advice is true or false.

Approaching the task

Before starting on the 'Approaching the task' activities, students could work in pairs or small groups to discuss what the editor will be looking for. Ask them to prepare a checklist of features the journalist should include in order to write a successful article. This checklist can then be used to support students as they work through Questions 1–3.

Read Question 4 to students and explain that they will be assessed on how well they put forward their view. The best responses will include reasons that are supported by evidence quoted from the text. Students should be sure to explain the significance of these quotations. Check that they know how to quote and revise this with them if they are unsure.

Give extra support by using Worksheet 2.4 for students to record their responses to Questions 1–3. If you think it is necessary, provide the following sentence stems to support their writing in response to Question 4:

- *The story is about…which will / will not engage/touch readers' hearts because…*
- *The online news report features the writer has included are…*
- *The writer has not included…*
- *The writer used…formal/informal English such as…This is effective / not effective because…*
- *Overall, I think the editor should / should not… because…*

Give extra challenge by asking students to devise a checklist for how to score highly when writing their response. If they make this in the form of a poster it can be presented to the class and then displayed while students attempt Question 4.

Reflecting on your progress

Questions 5 and 6 can be completed before or after the teacher has assessed the students' response to Question 4. If completed before, then students can present and label a 'before' and 'after' answer (i.e. their original answer and an improved version) so that the progress made in response to these activities can be monitored.

Note that if you are teaching these tasks *before* assessment, students will only improve aspects of their response that they can identify as being in need of improvement. In this case, it may be useful to read through the two responses with the annotations and comments, and then ask students to identify similar areas in their own response and to annotate these before making improvements. You could also emphasise that evaluating a student's current level is of secondary importance to the progress they can make during this session, and that this will be rewarded by the teacher afterwards.

If these tasks are to be completed *after* teacher assessment, then students can draw on the teacher's assessment comments to identify where improvements need to be made, as well as the example responses, annotations and comments.

Afterwards, students can work in pairs to peer-assess and confirm the improvements made. The writer should point out what things they noticed as the weaker elements in their first attempt and how they improved them. Alternatively, students could be asked to work independently to annotate their improved responses by identifying and labelling the changes they made, with an explanation of why what they have done is an improvement.

Use the Checklist for success on slide 3 to reinforce the points that students should include for a higher-level response.

Plenary	Hold a class discussion about the following points:
	• whether or not the editor should employ the journalist, giving reasons
	• what additional training the journalist needs in order to ensure that their writing is better targeted to audience and purpose when they are applying for future jobs.

2.5   Interviewing to gather news

Learning objectives
7SI1; 7SI3; 7SI5; 7SI7; 7SI8

Checkpoint progress test
* Paper 1, Section B

Differentiated learning outcomes
* **Lower: All students must** take part in a role-play interview.
* **Mid: Most students should** use words to show they are listening carefully to what someone is saying.
* **High: Some students could** use words and gestures to show they are listening carefully during the role-play.

Resources
* **Student Book**: pp. 46–47
* **Worksheet**: 2.5
* **PPT**: 2.5
* **Workbook links**: Unit 2.5, pp. 26–28

Introducing the skills

Make sure that students understand what an interview is, then ask them to suggest what kind of situations might require someone to interview another person, for example, for a job or a place in a school, television celebrity interviews, a newspaper reporter, a teacher investigating an incident at school.

Display PowerPoint 2.5 and use slides 1 and 2 to explore what would make this interview successful for the interviewer and the interviewee.

Give students time to decide on their good deed but also provide some examples. They should then complete Question 1.

Discuss body language, such as the appropriateness of extended eye contact, hand gestures, body positioning, and alert them to how the appropriateness of certain body language can vary in different cultures. Students should then practise their interviews for Question 2.

Give extra support by giving students Worksheet 2.5 to help them complete Question 1.

Give extra challenge by asking students to research different cultural norms relating to eye contact, or, if appropriate, to prepare two short role-plays demonstrating polite and less polite ways to ask and respond to questions.

Developing the skills

Students should develop and rehearse their interviews. They could work with another pair to listen and give feedback to each other as they attempt Question 3. For Question 4, draw out other suggestions from students. Similarly, develop Question 5 by asking students for other examples of helpful and unhelpful non-verbal communication.

Applying the skills

When students perform their interviews for Question 6, they can peer-review each other's efforts.

Plenary	Working to a time limit, first ask student pairs to agree their Top 10 tips for successful interviewing with another pair. Then join pairs to form larger groups that must agree their Top 10 tips. Continue combining groups until the final round, where the whole class is working together to create their final Top 10 tips.

Learning objectives
7Wa4; 7Wt1; 7Wt2

Checkpoint progress test
- Paper 1, Section B

Differentiated learning outcomes
- **Lower: All students must** plan a news story that will interest readers.
- **Mid: Most students should** plan the sequence of paragraphs to tell the news story in an interesting way.
- **High: Some students could** plan paragraphs and choose connectives to show how they link.

Resources
- **Student Book**: pp. 48–51
- **Worksheet**: 2.6
- **PPT**: 2.6
- **Workbook links**: Unit 2.6, p. 29

Introducing the skills

Read the task with students and make sure they understand that when faced with any task they should identify:

- the form that they should write in
- what content to include
- the purpose of the text
- the audience they need to suit.

Ask students to identify these in the task here. Then, in pairs, they could recap what the features of an online news report are, and discuss how they might best suit their (worldwide English-speaking) audience before feeding back to the class.

Some students may instantly know what they would like to write about, especially if they want to draw on the ideas developed in Topic 2.5. Reassure them that they can still benefit from doing the activities in this section as these model a process for developing ideas that they may find useful when faced with a more challenging task.

Make sure students understand the difference between 'general' and 'specific' before they begin Question 1.

In the initial stage, when generating ideas, students need to be thinking creatively rather than rationally. To help with this, encourage them not to pause to evaluate ideas, but to just make a quick note to capture the idea then move on to think up the next one. You can support this by setting a time limit of three minutes in which they should produce as many general 'good deed' suggestions as possible.

Afterwards, students should attempt Question 2, focusing on the advice given in the bullet points to refine their ideas more rationally. They should discard any that are unworkable and add details to those they can develop.

For Question 3, students could share possible ideas and evaluate which works best, suggesting improvements. They should then develop their plans independently during the remainder of Question 3, and in Questions 4 and 5.

Give extra support by using Worksheet 2.6 to support students' detailed planning from Question 3 onwards.

Developing the skills

Students should recap what they already know about writing in paragraphs. Alternatively you could display PowerPoint 2.6 to help students consolidate their understanding of paragraphs and think about how the whole text is organised.

When students move on to developing paragraph plans (beginning with listing points in Question 6, ordering them in Question 7 and developing detailed paragraph plans in Question 8), direct them to make notes rather than write in sentences.

Give extra challenge by asking students to consider how they will ensure that each paragraph suits their audience, for example, by including sufficient details, interesting information, variety of sentence structure.

Before Question 9, you could consolidate students' understanding of the different connectives and how they can be used by putting them in groups. Provide an opening sentence for a news story. Students then develop the story by taking it in turns to add the next sentence beginning with one of the connectives in the chart. Each connective can only be used once in each news story.

Applying the skills

After students have attempted Question 11, they can work in pairs to peer-evaluate their plans. Students should agree a suitable checklist by which to evaluate based on the learning from this lesson. For example:

✓ an engaging idea that will interest the audience

✓ planned content of the standfirst, middle paragraphs and final paragraph

✓ logical sequence of paragraphs

✓ inclusion of important details and people's views

✓ well-chosen connectives to link paragraphs.

Plenary	Students could make a flow chart explaining the planning process that they have followed during this lesson. If they need help creating this, draw up a template on the board with six blank boxes connected by downwards arrows.

Cambridge Checkpoint English
Stage 7

<table>
<tr><td>

Learning objectives

7Wp1; 7Wp4
</td><td>

Checkpoint progress test

- Paper 1, Section B
</td></tr>
</table>

<table>
<tr><td>

Differentiated learning outcomes

- **Lower: All students must** write a detailed simple sentence.
- **Mid: Most students should** use connectives to construct different types of sentences.
- **High: Some students could** craft sentences by choosing connectives to create an effect on their reader.
</td><td>

Resources

- **Student Book**: pp. 52–53
- **Worksheet**: 2.7
- **PPT**: 2.7
- **Workbook links**: Unit 2.7, p. 30
</td></tr>
</table>

Introducing the skills

Make sure that students fully understand the terms 'subject', 'verb' and 'object'. Then display several example sentences for them to identify these features before they attempt Question 1.

Explain that a standfirst is a paragraph that often consists of one single detail-packed sentence. Check students' knowledge of grammatical terms before using the grid to help them understand and then construct their own standfirst in Question 2.

Students can peer-assess each other's sentences, labelling each element using an agreed key (N for noun, PN for proper noun, A for adjective, and so on).

Give extra support by allowing students to use Worksheet 2.7 to help them construct sentences in response to Questions 2 and 3.

Developing the skills

Display PowerPoint 2.7. Use this to support the explanation of how different types of sentences are constructed, before students attempt Question 3. It is also helpful to show students the difference between using 'and' as a conjunction to join clauses and as a connective to add a final item to a list.

Give extra challenge by introducing the idea that the clauses in complex sentences can often be reversed so that the writer begins with the most engaging statement for the reader.

Applying the skills

To help students consciously craft their sentences in their response to Question 4, ask them to highlight their conjunction choices using different colours.

<table>
<tr><td>

Plenary
</td><td>
Write the four connectives and 'standfirst' on separate pieces of paper. Place them in a container. Organise students into competing teams, who take it in turns to suggest the topic to write about. Draw out a piece of paper and start the timer. The first team to construct an accurate sentence of the correct type about the topic scores 10 points, the second scores 5 points, and the third scores 1 point.
</td></tr>
</table>

Learning objectives
7Wp7

Checkpoint progress test
- Paper 1, Section B

Differentiated learning outcomes
- **Lower: All students must** understand the difference between direct and indirect speech.
- **Mid: Most students should** punctuate and express direct speech accurately in a report.
- **High: Some students could** punctuate and express both direct speech and indirect speech accurately in a report.

Resources
- **Student Book**: pp. 54–55
- **Worksheet**: 2.8
- **PPT**: 2.8
- **Workbook links**: Unit 2.8, pp. 31–32

Introducing the skills

Talk through PowerPoint 2.8 with students to help them understand the difference between direct and indirect speech.

Students can work in pairs to discuss and attempt Question 1, before working on Question 2 independently and then peer-assessing each other's efforts. Similarly, students should work independently to write their response to Question 3, but can peer-assess each other's efforts. Students may need reminding that they should use an apostrophe to abbreviate words when writing in informal language.

Give extra support by providing students with Worksheet 2.8 to respond to Questions 1 and 2 through annotation, so they can demonstrate their understanding more easily.

Give extra challenge by asking students to prepare a simpler list of instructions that could be used to teach a younger student how to accurately punctuate direct speech. Additionally, students can work in pairs to set their own versions of Question 2 for each other, and then assess them.

Developing the skills

Remind students that people often include reported speech in conversations when they tell someone about what another person has said. To reinforce this, ask students to tell you what the head teacher talked about in assembly. Write the exact words on the board and pick out the features of writing indirect speech. Students can then attempt Questions 4 and 5. They may need to be reminded that indirect speech is usually expressed in more formal English, without abbreviations.

Applying the skills

Students should attempt Question 6 on their own, but may peer-assess their outcomes.

Plenary	Assign appropriate gestures and/or sound effects to the punctuation needed to write direct speech accurately. Then give a student some direct speech to write on the board. Other class members can support the student as they write by making the appropriate gestures or sound effects to signal what punctuation is needed. Afterwards, all students can rewrite the direct speech as indirect speech.

Cambridge Checkpoint English Stage 7

Cambridge Checkpoint English
Stage 7

Learning objectives

7Wa4

Checkpoint progress test

• Paper 1, Section B

Differentiated learning outcomes

• **Lower: All students must** plan and write an online news report.

• **Mid: Most students should** organise their online news report effectively and include either direct or indirect speech.

• **High: Some students could** craft a well-organised online news report using connectives, direct speech and indirect speech effectively.

Resources

• **Student Book**: pp. 56–57

• **Worksheet**: 2.9

• **PPT**: 2.9

• **Workbook links**: Unit 2.9, pp. 33–34

Approaching the task

Recap with students what information they should identify when reading task instructions, for example, the required form, content, purpose and audience. Once they are clear on these, they could spend a few minutes in pairs noting the implications of those requested in the task by making a checklist of features to include. The whole class could then work together to draw up a checklist to display while students attempt the task.

Students could be given the opportunity to produce the final version of their text using ICT and the finished products used to create a class display.

Reflecting on your progress

This section of the topic could be used *before* students write their own piece to help them gain a thorough understanding of how they will be assessed and how to improve their writing. They can use the response examples as models for assessing their own work and can refer back to previous topics to consolidate their understanding. They can peer-check each other's evaluations before writing the improved versions. Afterwards, you can check both 'before' and 'after' versions to monitor their understanding and progress.

Alternatively, this section can be used *after* they have written and assessed their reports. You can then help them focus on the learning through the most relevant example, response and comments, as well as your own assessment of their work. After completing Questions 5 and 6, students can produce an improved version of their own article to self-assess before awarding themselves an improved level based on the 'Check your progress' points and the Checklist for success in PowerPoint 2.9.

Give extra support by allowing students to use Worksheet 2.9 to annotate Response 1.

Give extra challenge by asking students to work in pairs using progress points 4c–7c to annotate each other's articles, commenting on where effective skills have been used and suggesting improvements.

Plenary	Students could be given the opportunity to reflect on progress made during this session, and the sequence of lessons in this chapter by completing these four statements: • I am pleased that I have learned to… • The work I found most challenging was…because… • I would still like to practice… • To improve further, next I would like to learn how to…

Learning objectives
7Rv4; 7Wa4

Checkpoint progress test
• Paper 1, Section B

Differentiated learning outcomes

• **Lower: All students must** identify some features of a persuasive text.

• **Mid: Most students should** explain how positive adjectives are used in persuasive texts.

• **High: Some students could** recognise the features of a persuasive text and identify its purpose.

Resources

• **Student Book**: pp. 60–63

• **Worksheet**: 3.1

• **PPT**: 3.1

• **Workbook links**: Unit 3.1, pp. 35–36

Introducing the skills

Ask students to read the explanation of persuasive texts and texts that argue on page 60 of the Student Book. This could be read aloud. Establish that persuasive texts are used to promote a writer's point of view.

Ask students to work in pairs to answer Questions 1 and 2. Take brief feedback. The answers are:

1   The writer sympathises with the point of view that people enjoy going to zoos.

2   The word 'but' signals that the writer does not share this point of view.

Establish that in order to make a strong argument, writers need to consider the opposing view, and then undermine it.

Display slide 1 of PowerPoint 3.1, which shows the text from the newspaper article. Ask students to look at the words shown in red. They should work in pairs to explain to each other what these details in the text have in common and what they suggest about zoos.

At the end of the pair discussions, take class feedback and in a wider discussion build up to the point that the writer uses these words to hint at a negative opinion of zoos, by suggesting that they are old-fashioned and out of date.

Developing the skills

Ask students to work on their own to complete Questions 3, 4 and 5. Take brief feedback from individuals. The answers are as follows:

3   Text A = persuasive
Text B = argumentative
Text C = persuasive

4   The word choices are positive, e.g. 'stunning', 'biggest', 'amazing'.

5   The writer uses evidence to sound convincing.

Display slide 2 which contain Texts A, B and C. Ask less confident students to come up to the board and point out / explain the specific selection on the slide. Details that may help students with answering Questions 4 and 5 have been underlined on the slide. (The texts are also given on separate slides (3, 4 and 5) should you need to refer to them more closely.)

Read the two paragraphs below Question 5 on page 63. Ask students to identify which of the positive words in Texts A and C are adjectives. What other positive adjectives could the writers of these two texts have used to get across their point of view and persuade the reader? You could collate a list of suggestions on the board for students to refer to when completing the writing task at the end of the topic.

Remind students that statistics are a good form of evidence by showing them the example from Text B.

Applying the skills

Students should complete Question 6 on their own. As they write their website paragraphs, ask individuals to explain their choice of features and adjectives. How do they make the zoo sound appealing? The more they can describe and explain the purpose of their choices, the more likely it is that they will be able to transfer these skills to other types of writing.

Give extra support by allowing students to use Worksheet 3.1 to help scaffold their paragraph. Explain that they should plan their ideas using a spider diagram. They can add to the number of bubbles in the example if they need to. Students can then complete the cloze paragraph to organise their ideas.

Give extra challenge by asking students to write a second paragraph in which they use other persuasive features. Give them some examples of these other persuasive features: alliteration, the power of three and personal pronouns, for example. Explain these features if necessary.

Plenary	Ask students to look at the 'Checklist for success' on page 63 and identify which aspects from the list they have used. They should then look at the 'Check your progress' points and self-assess the level they are working at. Get students to identify areas in which they could improve. They could then rewrite their paragraphs to include any missing features.

<table>
<tr><td>

Learning objectives

7Ri1; 7Rv1

</td><td>

Checkpoint progress test

* Paper 2, Section A

</td></tr>
</table>

<table>
<tr><td>

Differentiated learning outcomes

* **Lower: All students must** identify the purpose of a persuasive text.
* **Mid: Most students should** comment on both the explicit and implicit meanings of words.
* **High: Some students could** link their comments about the explicit and implicit meanings of words to a writer's purpose.

</td><td>

Resources

* **Student Book**: pp. 64–67
* **Worksheet**: 3.2
* **PPT**: 3.2
* **Workbook links**: Unit 3.2, pp. 37–38

</td></tr>
</table>

Introducing the skills

Remind students that it is important to be able to identify both the obvious and the deeper meanings of words. This helps us understand a writer's viewpoint and the purpose of a text.

Students should work on their own to answer Question 1, then pair up to talk about the ideas they have come up with.

Display slide 1 of PowerPoint 3.2. Ask students to discuss in their pairs what the child says and what he really means. As a class, discuss why he does not ask for what he wants directly. Which words hint at what the child really wants (his purpose) and what he thinks (his viewpoint)?

Students should work in pairs to answer Questions 2–6. Take brief feedback. The answers are:

  2 'facing global extinction', 'threatened', 'in trouble'

  3 **a)** 'threatened'   **b)** 'massive'   **c)** 'unique'

  4 The new words make the tone urgent and insistent, so the zoo's work seems necessary and very important.

  5 The words 'threatened' and 'massive' are more emotive, and the word 'unique' makes the zoo seem like the only place that can help.

  6 The writer wants the reader to think the zoo is special and is doing vital work to help wildlife.

Direct students to play the following game to check their understanding of Questions 2–6. In small groups, they should take it in turns to say each of the following statements out loud. The other students need to identify whether they are true or false.

* The language in the text makes the zoo's work seem unimportant.
* The tone of the language is urgent and insistent.
* The tone of the language is light-hearted.
* The language in the text makes the zoo's work seem necessary and very important.
* The writer wants the reader to think the zoo is the same as other zoos.
* The writer wants the reader to think the zoo is special and is doing vital work to help wildlife.

Display slide 2, which shows definitions of *explicit* and *implicit meaning* and an explanation of *inference*. Make sure that students have fully grasped these concepts before moving on to the 'Developing the skills' section.

Give extra support by displaying slide 3. Ask students to work in pairs to identify the explicit and implicit meanings of the word 'towered'. (Explicit = the man is taller than the boy; implicit = the man is intimidating the boy.)

Cambridge Checkpoint English
Stage 7

Developing the skills

Display slides 4, 5 and 6 in turn. Spend some time with students looking at the sentence starters for Questions 7, 8 and 9. Ask them to identify which words show that they are writing about either the explicit or implicit meaning. For example, 'means' = explicit, 'hints' = implicit. Students should then complete Questions 7–9 independently.

When responding to Question 10, allow students to use a dictionary to help them check the definitions of explanations if necessary.

Give extra challenge by asking students to create their own sentence starters. This will help them become more independent when responding to texts. They could go on to write about the word choices from the texts in Topic 3.1 in a similar way. This will consolidate their understanding of the explicit and implicit meanings of a range of words.

After they have completed their work on the texts in Topic 3.1, they could create an activity based on what they have done for the rest of the students in the class to complete.

Applying the skills

Give students Worksheet 3.2 to help them plan their answer to Question 11. This will help students to break down the stages of analysis into manageable chunks before they write it up as a paragraph. This will support students who struggle to process information and/or find it hard to write in an extended way.

Plenary	Ask students to swap their paragraphs and check each other's work using the 'Checklist for success' and the 'Check your progress' points on page 67. Students should write:
	• *[Name] has checked your work.*
	• *You are working at Lower/Mid/High level because…*
	• *To improve, you need to…*

Cambridge Checkpoint English

Stage 7

3.3 | Using quotations as evidence

Learning objectives
7Rw1; 7Rv1

Checkpoint progress test
* Paper 2 Section A

Differentiated learning outcomes
* **Lower: All students must** choose a suitable quotation to support an idea.
* **Mid: Most students should** comment on the explicit and implicit meanings of the words in the quotation.
* **Higher: Some students could** select a range of quotations from a text and explain the effect of the writer's language.

Resources
* **Student Book**: pp. 68–69
* **Worksheet**: 3.3
* **PPT**: 3.3
* **Workbook links**: Unit 3.3, p. 39

Introducing the skills

Display the task on slide 1 of PowerPoint 3.3. Students should work in pairs to suggest what makes the penguin pool special. Encourage them to think about their word choices. When they have finished their discussions, show them slide 2 to reinforce the rules for punctuating and introducing quotations.

Read aloud the text describing 'Penguin Beach' from the Student Book. Ask students to identify what impression they get of it – for example, is it positive, negative, exciting, impressive, boring… Remind students that it is important to use quotations to back up their ideas.

Students then work in pairs to complete Questions 1–3.

Developing the skills

Direct students to work on their own to answer Questions 4 and 5. You could reinforce Question 4 by giving them Worksheet 3.3 and asking them to draw a continuum, from 'strong' to 'weak'. In pairs, they could then arrange the words 'even bigger spectacle' on the continuum. Take feedback from students and draw their attention to the fact that 'spectacle' is the most powerful word, so will therefore be the best one to write about.

Applying the skills

Students should work on their own to answer Question 6.

Give extra support by providing students with the sentence starters on slide 3 to help them structure their paragraph.

Give extra challenge by encouraging students to write about more than one powerful word that they can find in the 'Gorilla Kingdom' extract in the Student Book.

Plenary	Finish by asking students to write answers to the following questions in one minute. Time them as they write. Ask students to hand in their answers at the end. Then use their answers to help plan the next lesson, revisiting areas they are still struggling with. • What have you learned? • In what ways do you need further support?

Cambridge Checkpoint English
Stage 7

3.4

Responding to persuasive texts

Learning objectives	Checkpoint progress test
7Rw1; 7Rv1	• Paper 2, Section A

Differentiated learning outcomes

- **Lower: All students must** understand the purpose of a persuasive text and support an answer with a quotation.
- **Mid: Most students should** understand the explicit and implicit meanings of words and phrases, and explain the reasons for a writer's choice of vocabulary.
- **Higher: Some students could** explain the explicit and implicit meanings of words and link them to the writer's purpose, explaining the effect of quotations and giving reasons for their inferences.

Resources

- **Student Book**: pp. 70–73
- **Worksheet**: 3.4
- **PPT**: 3.4
- **Workbook links**: Unit 3.4, p. 40

Your task

Briefly recap the reading skills covered in Topics 3.1, 3.2 and 3.3. You could do this by asking students to work in pairs to prepare 30-second briefings. The presentation of these could be enlivened by challenging students to give their briefing in the manner of a well-known personality.

Remind students that it is important to recognise that some words have implicit as well as explicit meanings, and that they need to be able to comment on how these words can be used persuasively.

Display slide 1 on PowerPoint 3.4 and talk through the 'Checklist for success' to consolidate students' understanding before they start approaching the task.

Approaching the task

Ask students to read the text about orangutans. Then discuss the various strategies they might use to tackle words that they are not familiar with. Students should then complete Questions 1–4 on their own.

After they have worked through the question, get them to swap their answers with a partner. They should peer-assess each other's work using the 'Checklist for success'. Based on this, students should write a comment about their partner's response to Question 4 using the sentence starters on slide 2.

Give extra support by allowing students to refer back to earlier topics if they need to.

Reflecting on your progress

Questions 5 and 6 can be completed before or after you have assessed students' responses to Question 4. If completed before, then students can present and label a 'before' and 'after' answer (i.e. their original answer and an improved version) so that the progress made in response to these activities can be seen.

Note that if you are teaching these tasks before assessment, students will only improve aspects of their response that they can identify as in need of improvement. In this case, it may be useful to read through the two responses with the annotations and comments, and then ask students to identify similar areas in their response and to annotate these before making improvements. You could also emphasise that evaluating a student's current level is of secondary importance to the progress they can make during this session, and that this will be rewarded by the teacher afterwards.

If these tasks are to be completed *after* teacher assessment, then students can draw on the teacher's assessment comments to identify where improvements need to be made, as well as the example responses, annotations and comments.

Afterwards, students can work in pairs to peer-assess and validate the improvements made. The writer should point out what deficiencies they recognised in their first attempt and how they improved them. Alternatively, students could be asked to work independently to annotate their improved responses by identifying and labelling the changes they made with an explanation of why what they have done is an improvement.

Give extra challenge by asking students to use Worksheet 3.4 to create their own 'How does the writer use language' question, based on the extract. They should then either swap with a partner and answer this new question, or answer their own question.

Plenary	Finish by asking students to discuss what they have learned about using quotations and commenting on quotations. Monitor these discussions and guide students if necessary.

Learning objectives
7R01; 7SL1; 7SL6

Checkpoint progress test
N/A

Differentiated learning outcomes

- **Lower: All students must** express a viewpoint in a discussion.
- **Mid: Most students should** provide evidence to support their views and explain their reasons in a discussion.
- **High: Some students could** support others in a discussion by asking questions, summarising views and taking the initiative.

Resources

- **Student Book**: pp. 74–77
- **Worksheet**: 3.5
- **PPT**: 3.5
- **Workbook links**: Unit 3.5, p. 41

Introducing the skills

Display slide 1 from PowerPoint 3.5. Ask students to work in pairs to discuss the connections between the words in the word cloud. Which ideas do they think would be useful or interesting when discussing zoos or engendered species? Why?

Remind students that it is important to have researched a topic carefully before taking part in a formal discussion. Refer them to the grid on page 74 of the Student Book detailing the argument for and against zoos, and discuss the different ways in which ideas like this could be prepared – for example, as a grid, as bullet points, or as a spider diagram or mind map.

Direct students to work in pairs to answer Questions 1 and 2, then take brief feedback. The answers to Question 2 are:

Evidence 1: Animals suffer ill health and become unfit.
Evidence 2: Animals suffer stress and boredom.
Evidence 3: Zoos save endangered species.
Evidence 4: Zoos educate the public.

Work on Question 3 as a class discussion, eliciting the idea that the best way to persuade others of your point of view in a discussion is to provide strong evidence to back up the points you make.

Students should then work in the same pairs to answer Questions 4–6. You may wish to provide ICT access for students so that they can research facts and statistics for this topic. Alternatively, you could set Question 6 as a homework task for students to complete.

Give extra support by working with a small group of students, guiding them in working out that evidence is missing from the example response in Question 4.

Give extra support by pointing students towards the Evidence boxes in Question 2 to help them develop their responses to Questions 5 and 6.

Developing the skills

Display slide 2 from PowerPoint 3.5. Ask three students to read aloud the example as a script. In pairs or small groups, they should then draw up a list of strengths and weaknesses for this discussion.

Ask students to read through the information about the way to set up a discussion and the examples of good leadership skills for the chairperson at the start of the 'Developing the skills' section. Students should work in their pairs or small groups to answer Question 7. Take brief feedback from the class, and ask how well they think Lin, the chairperson, performed.

Students should then answer Question 8 on their own.

Organise the class into groups of three for Question 9. When they have finished their discussion on whether or not zoos should be banned, take feedback about the successes and difficulties that each group experienced. They could jot down notes about this while they are talking to help them remember.

Widen the discussion to take advice from different people on how these difficulties might be overcome.

Applying the skills

Students should work in groups of five to complete Question 10. If there are enough students in the class, then a sixth member of the group could take notes on how each member of the group fulfilled the criteria on the 'Checklist for success'.

Students could use the following sentence starters to help them structure their contributions:

- *I believe that…*
- *Clearly zoos…*
- *When I researched…I found out…*
- *For example…*
- *This tells us that…*
- *As a result, it is evident that zoos…*

Give extra support by providing students with Worksheet 3.5, which provides a series of prompts to help them provide informed responses.

Give extra challenge by providing a different question for discussion: *Should wild animals be kept as pets?* Remind students of the steps they should take when preparing their arguments and the rules for a good discussion.

 Plenary

Finish by asking students to get into groups and on a large shared piece of paper, create a spider diagram to show what they have learned about good discussions. Display slide 3 as an example. After five minutes, nominate one student from each group to feed back on one thing they have learned. At the end of the lesson, read through the students' responses to check their understanding of the topic.

Learning objectives
7Rw6; 7Wp4; 7Wp6; 7Wp7

Checkpoint progress test
• Paper 1, Section A

Differentiated learning outcomes
• **Lower: All students must** form complex sentences.
• **Mid: Most students should** create complex sentences for different effects.
• **High: Some students could** use complex sentences to create a wide range of effects.

Resources
• **Student Book**: pp. 78–79
• **Worksheet**: 3.6
• **PPT**: 3.6
• **Workbook links**: Unit 3.6, pp. 42–43

Introducing the skills

Remind students that it is important to vary sentences to create different effects in argumentative writing, and that complex sentences can be used to develop ideas.
If necessary, recap the structure of a complex sentence to ensure students fully understand how they are used.

Display slide 1 from PowerPoint 3.6. What do students notice about the sentences in the text? How could the text be improved? Get them to discuss this in pairs, and then share thoughts as a class.

In the same pairs, students should then answer Questions 1–3. To extend their practice on the use of conjunctions and prepositions, show them slide 2 and ask them to copy and complete the sentences using one of the words from the word bank on page 79 of the Student Book.

Developing the skills

Display slide 3. Use this to review the different places that a subordinate clause can be used in a sentence and then get students to try it out for themselves using the sentence on slide 4. Students then answer Question 4 on their own.

Before you get students to move on to the 'Applying the skills' section, give them Worksheet 3.6, which introduces adverbial clauses. This will help them think about further ways in which they can develop ideas in complex sentences.

Applying the skills

Students should complete Question 5 on their own.

Give extra support by helping students plan their arguments before forming them into complex sentences.

Give extra challenge by encouraging students to use adverbial clauses to make connections between the main idea and the supporting idea.

Display slide 5 and ask students to copy and complete three of the seven sentences to reflect their learning. Use these to reinforce any area of uncertainty in a class discussion.

3.7 Structuring an effective argument

Learning objectives
7Rv1; 7Wa4; 7Wt1; 7Wp6

Checkpoint progress test
- Paper 1, Section B

Differentiated learning outcomes
- **Lower: All students must** use signposting words to guide the reader.
- **Mid: Most students should** use connectives to show relationships between ideas in a series of paragraphs.
- **High: Some students could** structure a piece of argumentative writing, using connectives, evidence and reasons.

Resources
- **Student Book**: pp. 80–83
- **Worksheet**: 3.7
- **PPT**: 3.7
- **Workbook links**: Unit 3.7, pp. 44–45

Introducing the skills

Display slide 1 of PowerPoint 3.7 and ask students to discuss in pairs what would help someone find their way around a maze like this. Take feedback and link it to the introduction on page 80 of the Student Book, reminding students that it is important to *signpost* their writing so that the reader can follow the direction of their argument.

Read the text about endangered species around the class, and then give students enough time to work on their own to answer Questions 1–6. When they have finished, take feedback, focusing on the use of connectives and adverbs / adverbial phrases to signpost the argument.

As a class, look at the explanation and the grid of signposting words on page 82. How many of the signposting words did students identify?

Give extra challenge by asking students to identify *persuasive* devices. These might include personal pronouns, the rule of three and emotive language. Explain these devices using slide 2.

Developing the skills

Display slide 3, which provides a grid to help students complete Question 7. They should do this on their own.

In preparation for Question 8, guide students through the following steps:

1. Highlight the arguments in the grid that they think are strongest.

2. Which side have they highlighted the most arguments on (*for* or *against*)? This will be the side they support in their writing.

3. They should select the best three arguments for their chosen side. (These will go in paragraphs 1, 2 and 3, and then will be summed up in paragraph 6.)

4. Select one counter-argument, which they can prove wrong (for example, *it can be argued that zoos have beneficial breeding programs,* **however**, *these often lead to over-population of some species, due to pressures to breed 'cute' baby animals*. (This will go in paragraphs 4 and 5.)

When students have followed these steps, get them to complete their plan using the grid on page 83.

Give extra support by allowing students to use the internet or other resources to find suitable arguments and evidence to complete their planning grid.

Give extra challenge by asking students to plan arguments for a different topic: the pros and cons of keeping a wild animal as a pet, for example.

As they work, ask individual students why they have chosen to sequence their arguments in a particular way and whether they think their signposting phrases are appropriate. The more students can articulate their choices, the more they will be able to transfer these skills to other writing.

Applying the skills

Students should complete Question 9 on their own. If they are feeling confident, encourage students to use persuasive devices in their writing. Refer back to the text on pages 80–81 (for example, the final sentence in paragraph 3) to highlight examples of these devices in action. Refer also to the use of personal pronouns in the final paragraph of the extract. Students could use Worksheet 3.7 to practise identifying these features further before writing their own sentences.

Give extra support by working with students in a guided way to select possibilities for their writing. Remind them to begin paragraph 2 with a 'listing' signpost to signal it is their first argument (e.g. 'Firstly', 'First and foremost'). Take ideas from each student and direct them to look at the grid on page 82, if they are struggling to find an appropriate example. Refer to the text on pages 80–81 to further demonstrate to students how signposts should be used.

Plenary	Provide students with a sticky note or a small piece of card and ask them to answer the two questions below. They should hand them in at the end of the lesson. Use their responses to check if any material from this lesson needs to be revised before moving on. • How can you guide your reader when writing an argument? Give some examples. • Why is it important to do this?

Learning objectives

7Wa4; 7Wt1

Checkpoint progress test

- Paper 1, Section A

Differentiated learning outcomes

- **Lower: All students must** plan and write a letter to a newspaper.
- **Mid: Most students should** form complex sentences to create specific effects and use signposting words to link ideas between paragraphs.
- **High: Some students could** use a variety of different sentence structures and linking devices to create a range of effects in their letter.

Resources

- **Student Book**: pp. 84–87
- **Worksheet**: 3.8
- **PPT**: 3.8
- **Workbook links**: Unit 3.8, pp. 46–48

Your task

Recap with students what information they should identify when reading task instructions – for example, the required form, content, purpose and audience. Once they are clear on these, they could spend a few minutes in pairs noting the implications of those prescribed in the task by making a checklist of features to include. This could then form part of a whole-class collaboration to draw up a checklist, which can be displayed while students attempt the task.

Ask students to suggest any areas of learning they would like to revise before they begin work. Then display slide 1 of PowerPoint 3.8 and discuss with students the choice of signposting words and phrases, and the way the points have been sequenced. Ask students to decide in pairs whether (and if so, how) the order of points could be improved.

Take brief feedback, and then move on to discussing how the plan does not contain any evidence as it stands. Remind students that evidence is vital when writing a successful argument.

Approaching the task

Students should work through Questions 1–3 to start planning their letter. The task and a planning box for it are on Worksheet 3.8.

Give extra support by allowing students to work in pairs.

Display slide 2 and talk through the features used to make the opening two sentences engaging. Then direct students to complete Question 4 on their own. Students could then swap their openings and feed back to each other about ways to improve them.

Ask students what style of writing would be appropriate for a letter to a newspaper: formal or informal? Display slide 3 and ask students to discuss in pairs ways in which this sentence could be made more formal. Take feedback from students and rewrite the sentence in a more appropriate style.

Direct students to complete the assessment task, Question 5, on their own.

Give extra support by allowing students to have access to key chapters of the Student Book that they might need.

Give extra challenge by allowing students to write about a different topic, for example, 'argue for or against keeping wild animals as pets'; 'argue for or against keeping the local zoo open'; 'argue for or against a school trip to a local zoo'.

Reflecting on your progress

This section of the topic could be used before students write their own piece to help them gain a thorough understanding of how they will be assessed and how to improve their writing. They

Cambridge Checkpoint English
Stage 7

can use the response examples as models for assessing their own work and can refer back to previous topics to consolidate their understanding as necessary. They can peer-check each other's evaluations before writing the improved versions. Afterwards, you can check both 'before' and 'after' versions to monitor their understanding and progress.

Alternatively, this section can be used after they have written and assessed their letter. You can then help them focus on the learning through the most relevant example, response and comments, as well as your own assessment of their work. After completing Questions 6 and 7, students can produce an improved version of their own article to self-assess before awarding themselves an improved level based on the 'Check your progress' points on page 88 of the Student Book.

When they have completed Question 5, students could be given the opportunity to produce the final version of their text using ICT and the finished products could be used to create a class display.

Plenary	Students could be given the opportunity to reflect on progress made during this session, and the sequence of lessons in this chapter by completing these four statements: • I am pleased that I have learned to… • The work I found most challenging was…because… • I would still like to practise… • To improve further, next I would like to learn how to…

Learning objectives
7Rw1; 7Rw4; 7Wa4

Checkpoint progress test
* Paper 2, Section A

Differentiated learning outcomes
* **Lower: All students must** be able to identify some types of descriptive words.
* **Mid: Most students should** identify different descriptive words and techniques and consider their effect on the reader.
* **High: Some students could** recognise how a range of descriptive words and techniques achieve specific effects.

Resources
* **Student Book**: pp. 90–91
* **Worksheet**: 4.1
* **PPT**: 4.1
* **Workbook links**: Unit 4.1, p. 49

Introducing the skills

Ask students if they remember the function of nouns (naming an object), adjectives (describing a noun), verbs ('doing', 'being' or 'having' words) and adverbs (describing a verb). If students struggle with understanding the word classes, pick some of the highlighted words from the extract and ask them, for example, why 'gradually' is an adverb.

Ask students to work in pairs to answer Questions 1 and 2. Take feedback, discussing the effects of different words and showing how they can change the meaning of a description. Display slide 1 from PowerPoint 4.1 while going through the two tasks.

Developing the skills

Explain the three main types of imagery. Check students' understanding of the difference between a simile (a comparison using 'like' or 'as') and a metaphor (a comparison that describes something as if it is actually something else).

Ask students to work on Question 3. Then take brief feedback: simile ('like green skyscrapers'), metaphor ('scent poured from flowers') and personification ('linked hands and embraced'). After students have completed Question 4, talk through the possible effects. These might be: 'tall', 'imposing' (sentence 1); 'they are friendly', 'they look after each other' (sentence 2) (do not allow 'they are people' as this is always the case with personification); 'how strong the scent of the flowers is' (sentence 3).

Applying the skills

Students should complete Question 5 either in pairs or as a class using slide 2. Discuss Question 6 together, encouraging students to think about the use of additional senses (touch and sound) in the description. Ask students to complete Question 7 individually.

Give extra support by allowing students to use the writing frame on Worksheet 4.1.

Give extra challenge by asking students to evaluate which of their chosen techniques they feel is the most effective and why.

Plenary

Finish by holding a class discussion on what students have learned about descriptive words and the different effects they can have in a piece of writing.

Cambridge Checkpoint English Stage 7

Using quotations from descriptive writing effectively

Learning objectives
7Ri1; 7Rw1; 7Rw4; 7Rx1

Checkpoint progress test
* Paper 2, Section A

Differentiated learning outcomes
* **Lower: All students must** be able to select some words and phrases from a text that show what setting or atmosphere is like.
* **Mid: Most students should** select a range of words and phrases that show what setting or atmosphere is like.
* **High: Some students could** select a range of words and phrases, and begin to explain how they show what setting or atmosphere is like.

Resources
* **Student Book**: pp. 92–93
* **Worksheet**: 4.2
* **PPT**: 4.2
* **Workbook links**: Unit 4.2, p. 50

Introducing the skills

Make sure students understand what a quotation is and how they are demarcated using quotation marks (also called inverted commas or speech marks).

Ask students to work in pairs to read the text then answer Questions 1 and 2. Take feedback: a) false ('black sky'); b) true ('gasped'); c) false ('enormous'); d) false ('sparkling'); e) true ('like tiny ants'). If students find the task challenging, read through the text on slide 1 of PowerPoint 4.2, then work through the questions about it on slide 2 to secure the skills required for this topic.

Developing the skills

Point out to students that it is important to explain *why* you have chosen a specific quotation. Ask them to work in pairs on Question 3. You could model how this might be done with statement b), leading students to identify the most important part of the quotation (the verb 'gasped') and the effect this word has (suggests shock or something breath-taking).

Take brief feedback, pushing students to use technical language such as 'adjective' or 'simile'.

Give extra support by allowing students to complete this question as a card-sorting activity using Worksheet 4.2.

Applying the skills

Read the extract aloud and ask students to work through Question 4 on their own. Afterwards, discuss the effect of specific words, such as the adjectives 'dead', 'grey', 'motionless', 'dusty', the adverb 'hopelessly' and the phrases 'No birds sang' and 'no sign of any blade of grass'.

Give extra challenge by asking students to evaluate which word or phrase they felt was the most effective at creating a miserable atmosphere. Get them to explain their decision.

Plenary

Finish by asking students to explain why it is important to quote from a text and how quotations allow them to extend their responses to a text further.

Explaining how writers use different descriptive techniques

Learning objectives
7Rw2; 7Rw6; 7Rw7

Checkpoint progress test
- Paper 2, Section A

Differentiated learning outcomes

- **Lower: All students must** be able to find some different techniques that writers use in descriptive writing.
- **Mid: Most students should** identify some descriptive techniques and begin to explain why and how the writer has used them.
- **High: Some students could** select a range of descriptive techniques and explain why and how the writer has used them.

Resources

- **Student Book**: pp. 94–97
- **Worksheet**: 4.3
- **PPT**: 4.3
- **Workbook links**: Unit 4.3, pp. 51–52

Introducing the skills

Recap with students the importance of noticing and commenting on the different language techniques that writers use to reveal their ideas. Ask students if they can remember the four main word classes (verb, noun, adjective, adverb) and the three types of imagery (simile, metaphor, personification). Then introduce the idea of sounds, repetition and sentence types before reading the extract on page 94 of the Student Book aloud to the class.

Show students slide 1 of PowerPoint 4.3, which is an extended version of the grid on page 95. Ask them to copy this down (or give a printout of the slide to each pair). Students then work in pairs to answer Question 1, filling in the Example column. Take feedback. Answers might include:

- repetition = 'every' (in 'everything' and 'everyone'), 'servants'
- list = 'their eyes closed, their breathing slow, hoping...'
- short sentence = 'Violently.'
- onomatopoeia = 'whirred', 'rumble'.

Students should then return to their pairs to complete Question 2, filling in the last column in the grid.

Developing the skills

Discuss with students the importance of structuring a clear response, explaining the three bullet-point stages in the Student Book and applying them to the example response in Question 2.

Read through the extract from *A Game of Thrones*. Talk about the annotations provided with the text and make sure students understand each of these points. Explain terminology such as 'rhetorical question' if necessary. Then give students Worksheet 4.3 and ask them to complete Question 3 in pairs, annotating the text to show how it creates a harsh, wintry setting and develops an atmosphere of fear.

Take feedback, encouraging students to use technical language such as 'list' or 'repetition'. Ideas might include:

- The adjective 'quick' and the short sentence suggest urgency, as if Will is worried.
- The metaphor, simile and short sentence all create a powerful image of terror.
- The two verbs in the list suggest he is expecting danger.
- The short sentence emphasises the strangeness of the shadow's disappearance.
- Personification makes the trees sounds scary and aggressive.
- The verb 'freeze' (and later on, 'shivering') and the noun 'snow' remind the reader of the conditions.
- The short sentence emphasises the danger in not being able to see their enemy.
- The adverb 'so', followed by the short sentence, suggests that it is unusually cold, which implies danger.
- The single-sentence paragraph emphasises the danger, with the verb 'emerged' and the adjective 'dark' sounding sinister and threatening.

Cambridge Checkpoint English
Stage 7

Applying the skills

Ask students to complete Question 4 to show that they can structure a response to how the writer creates a harsh, wintry setting and develops an atmosphere of fear. Use slide 2 to remind students how to structure each paragraph.

Give extra support by helping students to select their strongest annotations and to follow the three-part structure for analysis.

Give extra challenge by asking students to select the points that they felt were most effective. Help them to include evaluative comments in their writing. You could give them sentence starters such as:

- *The most effective technique used by the writer was...*
- *This was particularly effective because...*
- *The writer made especially effective use of...*
- *In order to emphasise this, the writer used very effective...*

Plenary	Finish by asking students to share some of their three-part responses to the text. Encourage students who are sharing to improve their comments, either through more precise technical language or through more specific comments on the effects achieved. Ask students who are listening to identify how each response follows the three-part structure.

Differentiated learning outcomes

• **Lower: All students must** be able to find some different techniques that writers use in descriptive texts.

• **Mid: Most students should** identify different descriptive techniques and begin to explain why and how the writer has used them.

• **Higher: Some students could** select a range of descriptive techniques and explain why and how the writer has used them.

Resources

• **Student Book**: pp. 98–101

• **Worksheet**: 4.4

• **PPT**: 4.4

• **Workbook links**: Unit 4.4, pp. 53–54

Your task

Recap with students the different elements of analysing descriptive writing that they have covered in this chapter so far:

• word classes and techniques
• how to quote from a text
• how to make comments about the effects of specific words, techniques or sentence types
• how to write a response using a three-part structure.

Point out to students that in this topic they need to write a piece exploring the way that a writer has created setting and atmosphere in an extract. Then give students Worksheet 4.4 and ask them to complete the activity there to consolidate their understanding before they begin planning for the task.

Approaching the task

Read the extract aloud with students. You could read it to them, or it could be read around the class. Explain any difficult vocabulary.

Ask students to work through Question 1 on their own. Then take brief feedback of their ideas. They should then move on to Question 2, selecting the features about setting and atmosphere that they are going to explore.

Give extra support by helping students to select features that they fully understand and will feel confident writing about in detail. For example, students might find it accessible to write about the use of:

• negative adjectives to show how bad the setting is
('shattered', 'flooded', 'ruined')
• negative nouns to make the setting sound unclean and unwelcoming
('rats', 'vermin', 'thieves')
• powerful verbs to create an atmosphere of danger and unhappiness
('cannibalised', 'trapped').

Give extra challenge by encouraging students to select a range of different features, including language and structure, to comment on.

Before they move on to Question 3 and complete the extended writing task, show students slide 1 from PowerPoint 4.4, which highlights the sentence starters. Review these with the class. Ask students if they can come up with any other useful starters that might help them answer the question. Make a note of these on the board for students to refer to when writing.

Students should then complete Question 3 on their own.

Cambridge Checkpoint English
Stage 7

Reflecting on your progress

Questions 4 and 5 can be completed before or after you have assessed students' responses to Question 3. If completed before, then students can present and label a 'before' and 'after' answer (i.e. their original answer and an improved version) so that the progress made in response to these activities can be seen.

Note that if you are teaching these tasks before assessment, students will only improve aspects of their response that they can identify as in need of improvement. In this case, it may be useful to read through the two responses with the annotations and comments, and then ask students to identify similar areas in their response and to annotate these before making improvements. You could also emphasise that evaluating a student's current level is of secondary importance to the progress they can make during this session, and that this will be rewarded by the teacher afterwards.

If these tasks are to be completed *after* teacher assessment, then students can draw on the teacher's assessment comments to identify where improvements need to be made, as well as the example responses, annotations and comments.

Afterwards, students can work in pairs to peer-assess and validate the improvements made. The writer should point out the deficiencies that they recognised in their first attempt and how they improved them. Alternatively, students could be asked to work independently to annotate their improved responses by identifying and labelling the changes they made with an explanation of why what they have done is an improvement.

Display slide 2 while students are working on this section so they can refer to the 'Checklist for success' on slide 2 to help them at any point.

Give extra support by allowing students to work in pairs or in small groups with teacher input if necessary.

Give extra challenge by asking students to write an additional paragraph once they have completed their improved response, to develop their techniques.

Plenary	Finish by asking students to use the progress points to self-assess their extended reading work. Encourage students to note down **two** things that they have done well and **two** things that they could improve.

Learning objectives
7Wa7; 7Wa8

Checkpoint progress test
* Paper 2, Section B

Differentiated learning outcomes
* **Lower: All students must** be able to choose some specific adjectives and verbs for descriptions.
* **Mid: Most students should** use a variety of vocabulary and some imagery to create interesting descriptions.
* **High: Some students could** use a range of precise vocabulary and imagery to create interesting descriptions.

Resources
* **Student Book**: pp. 102–105
* **Worksheet**: 4.5
* **PPT**: 4.5
* **Workbook links**: Unit 4.5, pp. 55–56

Introducing the skills

Explain the importance of using varied vocabulary in order to create precise descriptions. Then read the short extract on page 102 of the Student Book.

Ask students to complete Questions 1 and 2 in pairs. Take brief feedback, discussing the words and phrases that they thought were successful (such as 'green cubes of jelly') and those that could be clearer or more precise (such as 'I really liked' or 'a bit like curry'). Try to get students to explore how some descriptions could be improved and which words and phrases raise questions in the reader's mind. Ask students to compile a list of questions that might find the answers. For example:

* Why did you 'really like' them?
* In what way did they taste 'a bit like curry'?

Ask students to complete Questions 3 and 4 in pairs. Review responses as a class, focusing in particular on why 'delicious' and 'spicy' are the most appropriate words to choose from the word bank. What effect do these words have on the reader?

Students should complete Questions 5 and 6 on their own. Afterwards, have some students read their rewritten pieces out loud to the class and talk about the different words students have chosen instead of 'said'.

Between Questions 5 and 6, use Worksheet 4.5 to extend students' interest in and understanding of synonyms. This is also an opportunity to get them to use a thesaurus effectively.

Developing the skills

Make sure students understand that varying descriptive words is not just a case of finding and using a synonym: it is important to select words that contain the *precise* meaning that you want to convey.

Ask students to complete Question 7, then talk as a class about why 'soaked', 'enormous' and 'deafening' were the best words to select from each list. For example:

* The 'deep puddles' that they 'splash' through would get them very wet so 'damp' or 'moist' is not strong enough. The word 'completely' suggests that 'soaked' would be most appropriate.
* The robot 'towers' over him so 'enormous' would be a more effective word than 'big' or 'large'. 'Plump' sounds wrong because it suggests a human who is a bit overweight.
* The word 'thundered' shows the word cannot be 'gentle' or 'soft'. 'Loud' would work but it is not as powerful as 'deafening'.

Put students into pairs to complete Question 8. Before they start, encourage them to discuss why the alternative words they are selecting from the word bank add greater meaning to the text.

Ask students to complete Questions 9 and 10.

Recap the idea of imagery with the class, reminding them of the work from earlier in the chapter. Complete Questions 11 and 12 together. Use slides 1 and 2 from PowerPoint 4.5 to aid class interaction.

Ask students to complete Question 13 on their own. Take feedback – students should be able to defend their choice, explaining why it is the most appropriate.

Explain the benefits of planning descriptive writing. Look at the photograph and spider diagram on page 105. Read through the descriptive writing about the cave and highlight where elements of the spider diagram have been used. Then ask students to complete Question 14.

Using slide 3, discuss which words would be suitable to describe a spacecraft and why. When students spot a word that does not seem suitable, they could suggest what sort of genre or setting the word would fit into (for example, 'tombstone' would fit in with a horror setting).

As a class, add to the list to create a word bank centred on the lexical field of a spacecraft.

Applying the skills

Draw students' attention to the 'Checklist for success', then ask them to complete Question 15 on their own.

Plenary	Ask students to swap their work with a partner. They should then peer-mark each other's descriptions, using the 'Check your progress' points. They should identify **two** things that their partner has done particularly well. Encourage the class to share their work aloud, telling listeners to try and identify particularly good descriptive words, phrases and techniques.

Learning objectives	Checkpoint progress test
7Wp2; 7Wp3	• Paper 2, Section B

Differentiated learning outcomes	Resources
• **Lower: All students must** be able to form some different sentence structures.	• **Student Book**: pp. 106–109
• **Mid: Most students should** use some different sentence structures to create specific effects.	• **Worksheet**: 4.6
• **High: Some students could** use a variety of different sentence structures to create a wide range of effects.	• **PPT**: 4.6
	• **Workbook links**: Unit 4.6, pp. 57–58

Introducing the skills

Emphasise the importance of using varied sentence structures to convey information and engage the reader effectively. Explain that this topic looks at some of the different types of sentence structure and how each one can be used in descriptive writing.

Read the short extract of descriptive writing and, using Questions 1 and 2, discuss with students what is wrong with only using very short sentences.

Using the examples in the Student Book, explain the difference between simple and compound sentences. Check students' understanding by asking them to complete and then feed back on Question 3. To consolidate their learning, ask students if they can break up the following compound sentences into simple sentences:

- The girl was crying because she had lost her favourite toy.
- The shop was brightly lit and it sold all sorts of fantastic gadgets.

Referring to the example in the Student Book, explain how a string of simple sentences can be turned into longer compound sentences. Check students' understanding by asking pairs to complete and feed back on Question 4.

Using the extract and task in Question 5, ask students if they can see why the simple sentence has been used (to create impact, shock or surprise). Explain that simple sentences should only really be used to create a specific effect.

Developing the skills

Using the example at the top of page 108, explain how a complex sentence is constructed. Highlight the importance of using commas to separate the main information (or main clause) from the extra information (the subordinate clause). Tell students that the way to check that the comma is in the right place is to see if the main information makes sense on its own (whereas the extra information will not make sense). For example:

Looking through the window, <u>the man saw his dog come racing across the road</u>.

If the comma was in the wrong place, there is no main clause that makes sense:

Looking through the window the man saw, his dog come racing across the road.

Use Question 6 to secure these ideas. Students could be encouraged to say the different parts of the sentence aloud as this may help them to clarify which part makes sense on its own.

Students should have identified the main information as:

- **a)** We thought it was dangerous to stop and eat.
- **b)** We decided to seek shelter in an abandoned building.
- **c)** The whole city was silent.

If necessary, as a class say the parts that do not make sense aloud and discuss why this is. For example, 'Even though we were starving' sounds incomplete: it needs more information for it to make sense.

To extend students' understanding, you could use the slides in PowerPoint 4.6 to explore complex sentences and the movement of the subordinate clause.

Ask students to complete Question 7 in pairs, using the word bank of conjunctions from the start of the section. Take brief feedback. Make sure students understand that they cannot just choose any conjunction: it must convey the correct information that matches what is happening in the story.

Explain that you are now going to start exploring in more depth the specific effects that writers can achieve through different sentence structures. Read through the extract from *A Game of Thrones* and ask students to complete Question 8 in pairs.

Take brief feedback. The answers are:

a) the first sentence
b) the second sentence
c) the third sentence.

Ask students to complete Questions 9 and 10. When they have done so, hold a class discussion about the effect of the extra information: why does it make a story more interesting to read when you have these additional details, and what is a story like without them?

Applying the skills

Read through the 'Checklist for success' to remind students of the different skills covered in this lesson. Then ask them to complete Question 11 on their own.

Linking back to the previous topic, you could encourage students to use a spider diagram for initial planning, but remind them to focus on employing a range of sentence structures for effect.

Give extra support by allowing students to use the writing frame on Worksheet 4.6.

Give extra challenge by encouraging students to combine their use of sentence structures with their previous learning about descriptive words and phrases.

Plenary	Ask students to swap their work with a partner. They should then peer-assess each other's descriptions, using the 'Check your progress' points, and identify two things that their partner has done particularly well in terms of sentence structures.
	Afterwards, encourage a few students to come up – one at a time – and write one of their complex sentences on the board but without the correct punctuation (either missing out the comma or deliberately putting it in the wrong place). Challenge the rest of the class to find and correct each error.

Learning objectives
7Wt1; 7Wt2

Checkpoint progress test
- Paper 2, Section B

Differentiated learning outcomes
- **Lower: All students must** be able to plan paragraphs that each has a different focus.
- **Mid: Most students should** plan and use paragraphs for different effects.
- **High: Some students could** plan and use paragraphs for a range of effects and use prepositions for precision.

Resources
- **Student Book**: pp. 110–113
- **Worksheet**: 4.7
- **PPT**: 4.7
- **Workbook links**: Unit 4.7, pp. 59–60

Introducing the skills

Recap the main function of paragraphs and then read the extract from *The First Men in the Moon*. Ask students to complete Questions 1, 2 and 3 in pairs. When they have done so, discuss the answers:

1. The writer introduces a sound at the end of the first paragraph.
2. The second paragraph describes the sound through the use of onomatopoeia.
3. The third paragraph builds up the reader's understanding of the sound and refers again to the surroundings.

Referring to the bullet points below Question 3, explain how the writer has used each paragraph to achieve a different effect for the reader.

Students should then return to their pairs to complete Questions 4 and 5. Take brief feedback. Responses might include:

4. The reader is told that everything looks the same; we get some details of their surroundings including the weather; we are told that the sameness was disorientating.
5. We are told that the sound is low and a long way away; it is a regular and powerful beat; it astonishes them, creates a mysterious atmosphere and affects their view of their surroundings.

Explain that, having explored some ways in which writers use paragraphs, students are now going to try writing some of their own. Before they begin, give them some time to look carefully at the picture on page 111, noticing the details.

They should then complete Question 6, creating a spider diagram to record those details based on the template in the Student Book or slide 1 in PowerPoint 4.7. Remind students they can add as many 'bubbles' as they like to record all their ideas.

Take brief feedback to make sure everyone has plenty of ideas. Then ask them to work on Question 7 on their own, turning their spider diagram into a descriptive plan. They can complete the grid on Worksheet 4.7 to help with this.

Ask students to share their plans in small groups, discussing the ways in which they have divided their ideas up and identifying any problems.

Developing the skills

Using the Student Book, explain that it is important to organise ideas *within* (not just into) paragraphs. Prepositions are a key element of how to achieve this. To practise prepositions, write the following brief paragraph on the board, without the prepositions and see if students can fill them in using the word bank in the Student Book:

There was a piece of cheese [on] the floor [under] the table. A mouse was hiding [behind] the door but then it came [inside]. There was a cat [between] the mouse and the cheese. It towered [above] the mouse. When the mouse tried to get [around] the cat, the cat pounced [upon] it and gobbled it up.

Ask students to work in pairs on Question 8 or complete it as a class using slide 2.

Then ask students to complete Question 9 in pairs. Take brief feedback, encouraging students to share their sentences whilst others in the class identify the prepositions.

Applying the skills

Read through the 'Checklist for success' to remind students of the different skills covered in the lesson. As a fun way to remind students of the different elements that make up a good piece of writing, play 'writing skills bingo'. Ask students to make a grid of six boxes and to write a different feature of good writing into each box. Then read out the following techniques at random:

full stop + capital letter	correct spelling	prepositions
description	imagery	complex sentences
short sentences	compound sentences	paragraphs
simile	metaphor	personification
varied vocabulary	different senses	correct punctuation

The first student to cross off all their features is the winner.

Students should then complete Question 10 on their own.

Give extra support by helping students to decide which paragraph to write up and where they might use prepositions in their writing.

Give extra challenge by encouraging students to use prepositions effectively whilst also drawing on the skills of vocabulary and sentence structure developed in previous lessons.

Plenary	Give each pair of students a preposition from the word bank in the Student Book that they used earlier. Pick students to read out their work. Each time the students' designated preposition is read out, they must stand up or raise their hand.
	Afterwards, discuss whether students have used a variety of prepositions to make their work more interesting and, if not, how they could make small alterations to their work to achieve this.

Learning objectives
7Wt1; 7Wt2

Checkpoint progress test
* Paper 2, Section B

Differentiated learning outcomes
* **Lower: All students must** be able to use some descriptive techniques.
* **Mid: Most students should** use a range of descriptive techniques.
* **High: Some students could** use a full range of language and structure techniques to create engaging descriptive writing.

Resources
* **Student Book**: pp. 114–117
* **Worksheet**: 4.8
* **PPT**: 4.8
* **Workbook links**: Unit 4.8, pp. 61–62

Your task

Recap on the different descriptive writing skills that students have built up from this chapter:

* varied vocabulary (including imagery and consideration of synonyms)
* varied sentence structures (and the different effects they can achieve)
* organising ideas into and within paragraphs.

Once they are clear on these, they could spend a few minutes in pairs noting the implications of those prescribed in the task by making a checklist of features to include. This could be part of a whole class collaboration to draw up a checklist, which can be displayed while students attempt the task.

Read through the task and explain how it aims to assess the writing skills that they have just recapped. Ask students to suggest any areas of learning they would like to revise before they begin work.

Approaching the task

Ask students to work through Questions 1 and 2 on their own, using Worksheet 4.8 to plan their ideas.

Students should also complete Question 3. This could be done on the back of Worksheet 4.8 so all their planning and preparation work is together.

Show students slide 1 in PowerPoint 4.8. Discuss the importance of a striking opening sentence in descriptive writing. Go through the opening sentences on the slide and ask students which one they find most effective. Why? Ask if they think any of them could be improved and, if so, how?

Look at slide 2 and get students to think about how the writer has tried to make this sentence striking for the reader. They should consider sentence structure and word choices.

Students then complete Question 4, creating their own striking opening.

Give extra support by helping students to choose what they want to begin their story with (by selecting a feature of their plan, for example, a building or a feature of the landscape). Then help them to select words that are striking. Either discuss what they want to write then help them use a thesaurus to come up with good words, or ask them to write down their sentence and then underline key words for them that they should try to alter.

Give extra challenge by encouraging students to think of an opening that is striking yet also unusual or unexpected. Push them to deliberately use language, structure and/or specific descriptive techniques in an interesting and engaging way.

Cambridge Checkpoint English
Stage 7

Take brief feedback on their opening sentences. Encourage the class to comment on what is engaging about each opening sentence, as well as how it might be improved.

Ask students to complete the extended writing task. Referring to Question 5, remind them of the benefits of spending five minutes at the end checking their work for errors.

Reflecting on your progress

This section of the topic could be used before students write their own piece to help them gain a thorough understanding of how they will be assessed and how to improve their writing. They can use the response examples as models for assessing their own work and can refer back to previous topics to consolidate their understanding as necessary. They can peer-check each other's evaluations before writing the improved versions. Afterwards, you can check both 'before' and 'after' versions to monitor their understanding and progress.

Alternatively, this section can be used after they have written and assessed their descriptions. You can then help them focus on the learning through the most relevant example, response and comments, as well as your own assessment of their work. After completing Questions 6 and 7, students can produce an improved version of their own article to self-assess before awarding themselves an improved level based on the 'Check your progress' points.

Give extra support by allowing students to work in pairs or as small groups with teacher input. In particular, discuss with students how they are using varied vocabulary or a range of accurately punctuated sentence structures.

Give extra challenge by asking some students to add an additional paragraph once they have improved the response. Encourage students to think about writing techniques that they have not already used and that they could incorporate into their paragraph in order to broaden the range of skills that they are displaying. For example, more detailed imagery or complex sentences where the subordinate clauses are in different places (so rather than the subordinate clause always coming before the main clause, it could sometimes be after and sometimes be in the middle).

Plenary  Look at slide 3 and the Checklist for success. Ask students to get into teams of three or four. Each time you read one of the ideas on the checklist, students should look through their creative writing from the lesson and find a good example of the feature in use. This should be shared with the rest of the class, discussing whose example is the most effective and why.

What is narrative writing?

Learning objectives

7Rv2; 7Rv3; 7Wa8

Checkpoint progress test

* Paper 2, Section A

Differentiated learning outcomes

* **Lower: All students must** distinguish between narrative and non-narrative texts.
* **Mid: Most students should** understand the main features of narrative texts.
* **High: Some students could** understand and explain in detail the features of narrative openings.

Resources

* **Student Book**: pp. 120–121
* **Worksheet**: 5.1
* **PPT**: 5.1
* **Workbook links**: Unit 5.1, p. 63

Introducing the skills

Explain to students that most books are either *narrative* or *non-narrative* texts. The two types can be identified by particular features. Narrative texts are stories, whereas non-narrative texts often use lists, tables or images to convey information. When students have read the opening information, give them Worksheet 5.1 and ask them to draw up a quick summary list of the different features of the two text types.

Ask students to complete the grid for Question 1 at the bottom of Worksheet 5.1. Then display slide 1 of PowerPoint 5.1 and ask them to check their answers. Discuss in more detail any that they got wrong. Explain that identifying different types of texts will help them choose the best way of getting their message across in their own writing.

Developing the skills

Read the extract on page 121 aloud to the class. Ask students to discuss Question 2 in pairs, then feed back to the class (they should come up with words such as 'confused', 'scared' and 'agitated').

Ask students to read the information about story arcs, and then answer Questions 3–5 in pairs. Answers include 'the letter that changed her world', 'the slim nose with the diamond stud' and 'they'd changed her identity and given her a new life'.

Give extra support by displaying slide 2, which contains tips on some details students should look for to help them find the details required for Questions 3, 4 and 5.

Give extra challenge by asking students to identify the genre of the story and give evidence for their suggestion.

Applying the skills

Students should complete Question 6 on their own. As they work, ask individual students what details they have identified as important. Encourage them to use evidence from the text to support their answers.

Plenary	Ask students for verbal feedback on each of the points in Question 6. They should quote evidence from the text wherever possible. Discuss any differences in the answers students may have come up with.

Cambridge Checkpoint English
Stage 7

Identifying how writers communicate ideas in stories

Learning objectives	Checkpoint progress test
7Ri1; 7Rw1; 7Rv1	• Paper 2, Section A

Differentiated learning outcomes

- **Lower: All students must** identify words that communicate ideas.
- **Mid: Most students should** identify words and phrases that create characters.
- **High: Some students could** explain how a writer has created suspense.

Resources

- **Student Book**: pp. 122–123
- **Worksheet**: 5.2
- **PPT**: 5.2
- **Workbook links**: Unit 5.2, p. 64

Introducing the skills

Explain that the words and phrases a writer chooses are very important in making their meaning clear. Ask students to work in pairs to answer Question 1. They could do this verbally or they could work together to create a spider diagram in their books. When they have finished, take brief feedback.

Give extra support by giving students Worksheet 5.2 to help frame their answer to Question 1. Once they have chosen appropriate adjectives to describe the house, they should complete the grid to explain their choices and, if possible, come up with three more of their own.

Give extra challenge by asking students to use the adjectives they have come up with to write a paragraph describing an old, run-down building.

Read the extract on page 122 aloud around the class. Then ask students to answer Question 2 with a show of hands.

Display slide 1 of PowerPoint 5.2, which contains the extract, and select students to pick out words and phrases to answer Question 3.

Developing the skills

Display slide 2 and talk through the definitions of different narrative viewpoints. Identify examples of Cecily's viewpoint in the extract. Students should then complete Question 4 in small groups.

Give extra challenge by asking students to find words and phrases from earlier in the extract to support and strengthen their ideas.

Applying the skills

Ask one student to read the extract. Students should answer Question 5 on their own.

Plenary	Students should swap their sentences with a partner and peer-assess each other's work using the 'Checklist for success' and the 'Check your progress' points. When they have finished, hold a class discussion to consolidate the skills students have learned about identifying ideas and themes in a text.

5.3 Creating characters

Learning objectives

7Ri1; 7Rw1; 7Wa2; 7Wa3; 7Wp2; 7Wp3

Checkpoint progress test

* Paper 2, Question A

Differentiated learning outcomes

* **Lower: All students must** describe characters using adjectives.
* **Mid: Most students should** use different adjectives to describe contrasting characters.
* **High: Some students could** describe contrasting characters and show the relationship between them.

Resources

* **Student Book**: pp. 124–125
* **Worksheet**: 5.3
* **PPT**: 5.3
* **Workbook links**: Unit 5.3, p. 65

Introducing the skills

Ask students to look at the picture on page 124 in the Student Book and, in pairs, come up with a list of adjectives in answer to Question 1. Take brief feedback – they might come up with words such as 'confident' for character and 'tall' for appearance.

Show students the extract on slide 1 of PowerPoint 5.3 and ask them to think about Question 2 independently. Take feedback by asking students to underline key phrases on the board and explain why they are important. Students should then answer Question 3 in pairs and offer brief feedback to the class.

Developing the skills

Ask students to read the next extract, then answer Question 4 on their own. When they have finished, they should complete Worksheet 5.3 to consolidate their thinking about the effect of different adjectives. When students have around five adjectives in each column, get them to complete Question 5.

Give extra challenge by asking students to describe Sloan's character, using evidence from the extract. Display slide 2 to guide students on the type of details they should be looking for.

Ask students to answer Question 6. When they have three phrases, get them to swap work with a partner. The partner should choose their favourite phrase and write a brief comment explaining their choice.

Give extra support by working with students in a guided way to suggest possibilities.

Give extra challenge by asking students to write in extended sentences, using connectives and adding as much detail as possible.

Applying the skills

Ask students to answer Question 7 using the skills they have learned in the previous activities.

Plenary	To consolidate understand of adjectives, play 'adjective tennis' around the class. Give students different adjectives and ask them for an opposite. Start with 'kind/mean' or 'gentle/rough'. Make sure that everyone has at least one go.

Cambridge Checkpoint English
Stage 7

Learning objectives
7Rw1; 7Wp2; 7Wp3

Checkpoint progress test
- Paper 2, Section A

Differentiated learning outcomes
- **Lower: All students must** recognise words that create setting.
- **Mid: Most students should** understand how adjectives create character through description of setting.
- **High: Some students could** comment on how setting reveals a character's mood.

Resources
- **Student Book**: pp. 126–129
- **Worksheet**: 5.4
- **PPT**: 5.4
- **Workbook links**: Unit 5.4, pp. 66–67

Introducing the skills

Explain to students that settings are very useful for writers. They use them to reveal information about characters and situations, as well as to create the *mood* of a story. Remind students that the mood is how the story makes the reader feel. This is often influenced by *tone*, which can include the way the narrator describes the setting.

Ask students to complete Question 1 on their own. Take feedback by asking individual students to write a word on the board and explain their choice. Answers are 'gleaming', 'soft', 'peaceful' and 'pearly'.

Give students Worksheet 5.4 and ask them to complete the cloze paragraph, using adjectives of their own choosing, to consolidate their understanding of how word choice creates setting.

Ask students to answer Question 2 in pairs. They could make a note of the words they choose and start to build semantic fields of words that create certain atmospheres.

Give extra support by showing students slide 1 of PowerPoint 5.4, which contains a list of words that they could choose from to describe the forest. Good words to use to present it as mysterious and frightening might be 'dark', 'hidden' and 'brooding'.

Ask students to read the extract from *Eragon*. This could be read aloud. Ask them to write out their answer to Question 3 on their own and then share it with a partner. Take one suggestion from each pair as feedback (answers should be 'exciting', 'curious', 'apprehensive' or similar).

Students should then complete Question 4 independently.

Developing the skills

Explain that setting can also tell the reader a lot about characters. The type of place in which a character lives gives clues about what kind of person they are. Similarly, the way a character sees places and reacts to them gives the reader an insight into their thoughts and feelings.

Read the extract on page 127 of the Student Book aloud with students, and then split them into small groups to work on Question 5. When they have finished, take one point from each group as feedback. Answers should use 'mysterious' and suspicious', rather than 'gentle' or 'friendly'. Encourage students to explain their choice.

Give extra support by working with smaller groups of students in a guided way to suggest possibilities.

Give extra challenge by asking students to come up with their own words, as well as using the word bank.

Still in their groups, ask students to consider Question 6. Take feedback with a show of hands. Most students will answer 'no'. You could extend this by encouraging students to play devil's advocate – get them to try and think of ways in which a kind and welcoming person might end up living in a place like this.

Applying the skills

Ask students to read the extract on page 128. This could be read aloud round the class. Ask individual students to pick out words or phrases they are unsure of and have a class discussion about their meaning and effect. Encourage students to use the vocabulary list to enhance their understanding. Then ask students to identify words and phrases they find particularly effective. Discuss these as a class.

Before students begin Question 7, show them slide 2, which contains statements about the text. Select students to come to the board and choose the sentences they think are the most accurate and helpful. (Sentences 1, 4 and 5 are helpful; sentences 2 and 3 are simplistic and misleading.)

Students should then complete Question 7 on their own. As they work, circulate round the room and ask individual students to discuss their responses to the bullet points with you. Encourage them to add extra detail and evidence from the text, as this will help them improve the quality of their writing.

Take feedback on each section of the question from individual students. Ask others in the class to pick out one point that was strong, and one that could be developed or extended.

Give extra challenge by asking students to write a contrasting description to show what the character expected the house to be like.

Plenary	Writers often use setting to help us to understand the characters in a piece of writing. The setting in the extract prepares the reader for the character that lives there. Ask students to close their eyes, then read the description aloud to them. Ask them to try to visualise approaching the house and opening the door. What kind of person do they expect to find?
	Ask students to write on three sticky notes three adjectives that describe the person who lives in the house. They should come up with answers along the lines of 'lonely', 'sad' and 'isolated'.
	Now ask each student to choose their preferred adjective and stick it on the board at the front of the room. Select three students to explain their choice.

Understanding story structure

Learning objectives
7R02; 7Rv2

Checkpoint progress test
* Paper 2, Section A

Differentiated learning outcomes
* **Lower: All students must** explain why readers choose particular types of writing.
* **Mid: Most students should** plan a story based on an end goal.
* **High: Some students could** structure a story with obstacles and an end goal.

Resources
* **Student Book**: pp. 130–131
* **Worksheet**: 5.5
* **PPT**: 5.5
* **Workbook links**: Unit 5.5, p. 68

Introducing the skills

Explain to students that writers structure their stories carefully to keep their readers interested and entertained. Problems and important goals keep readers interested.

Ask students to read the information about the structure of a story arc on page 130 of the Student Book. To ensure they have fully understood the content of each section, give them Worksheet 5.4 and ask them to fill in the flow diagram with bullet points listing the kind of information that each part of the story might contain. Encourage them to think beyond the summary in the Student Book and to list one or two additional features that might characterise the beginning, middle and end of a story.

Ask students to discuss Question 1 in pairs. Take brief feedback from each pair. Check that they have identified obstacles as part of the plot, rather than simply unfortunate aspects of a character's situation.

Ask students to answer Question 2 independently and then compare answers in small groups. If they have come up with different orders, they should be able to justify their choices. You could ask them to decide on their preferred order.

Give extra challenge by asking students to put the obstacles they have identified in a narrative order. There is no set answer for this task, but discussing possible answers will develop understanding of narrative structures.

Developing the skills

Display PowerPoint 5.5, which shows a number of different genres and end goals. Use this as a starting point for a class discussion around Question 3. Students could state their preference (or circle it on the board) and briefly explain their choice. They can choose more than one if they like.

Give extra support by naming some books from different genres that students might be familiar with, to reinforce the kind of story they can expect in each genre.

Applying the skills

Ask students to answer Question 4 independently and then present their timelines to one another in small groups.

Plenary	Ask one student from each group to feed back to the class on the most effective story structure presented in their group. They should be able to explain why this would appeal to readers.

Learning objectives

7Ri1; 7Rw1; 7Rw8; 7Rv1; 7SL1; 7SL3; 7SL7; 7SL8

Checkpoint progress test

- Paper 2, Question A

Differentiated learning outcomes

- **Lower: All students must** summarise the events in a narrative text.
- **Mid: most students should** explain what words and phrases make the narrative interesting.
- **High: some students could** comment on structure and how it creates suspense.

Resources

- **Student Book**: pp. 132–135
- **Worksheet**: 5.6
- **PPT**: 5.6
- **Workbook links**: Unit 5.6, pp. 69–71

Your task

Briefly recap the reading skills covered in this chapter. You could do this by asking students to work in pairs to prepare 30-second briefings describing the features of narrative texts.

Explain to students that they will write a short review summarising a novel extract and explaining why their friends should read it.

Ask students to read the extract on pages 132–133 of the Student Book. They could do this alone or you could read it around the class, clarifying any difficult vocabulary as you go. Check students' understanding of the passage by asking them to summarise the events of each paragraph in single sentences.

Show slide 1 of PowerPoint 5.6. Ask students to come to the board and underline the words and phrases that they find interesting. Discuss these as a class. They may choose 'barren', 'shreds' or 'skeletons', but other responses are valid as long as the student can explain why they find them interesting. Explain that these 'interesting' words and phrases are the ones that they may wish to focus on or use as evidence to support their ideas in their review.

Approaching the task

Ask students to work in pairs to answer Questions 1–4. Take brief feedback. Answers might include:

1 The castle is mysterious.

2 'He replaced the sword: it was too heavy to be of use'.

3 Skeletons are associated with death and decay, so the wall hangings are obviously old and worn.

4 Whose is the singing voice? Why has the castle been abandoned? What is the mark of the sword? How did Roland's ball end up in the castle?

To consolidate their understanding before they write their review in Question 5, give students Worksheet 5.6, which contains a different extract from the passage. Ask them to underline the words and phrases that indicate that this is a mysterious setting. They should then annotate these to explain what they find effective about these words. Encourage students to use the terminology they have come across in the chapter so far.

Students should then answer Question 5 on their own. If you feel they need extra support, show them slide 2, which contains some scaffolded sentence starters. Once students have responded to each of the three headings, ask them to move on to the 'Reflecting on your progress' section.

Cambridge Checkpoint English
Stage 7

Give extra support by offering students targeted support and guidelines for their review if they need it. Remind them to look for interesting words and phrases. Ask them what 'grabs' them about the extract.

Give extra challenge by asking students to draw up a chart of nouns, adjectives and verbs the writer uses that make the description interesting. They could add this to the semantic fields they began creating in Topic 5.4.

Reflecting on your progress

Questions 6 and 7 can be completed before or after you have assessed students' responses to Question 5. If completed before, then students can present and label a 'before' and 'after' answer (i.e. their original answer and an improved version) so that the progress made in response to these activities can be monitored.

Note that if teaching these tasks *before* assessment, students will only improve aspects of their response that they can identify as being in need of improvement. In this case, it may be useful to read through the two responses with the annotations and comments, and then ask students to identify similar areas in their response and to annotate these before making improvements. You could also emphasise that evaluating a student's current level is of secondary importance to the progress they can make during this session, and that this will be rewarded by the teacher afterwards.

If these tasks are to be completed *after* teacher assessment, then students can draw on the teacher's assessment comments to identify where improvements need to be made, as well as the example responses, annotations and comments.

Afterwards, students can work in pairs to peer-assess and confirm the improvements made. The writer should point out what things they noticed as the weaker elements in their first attempt and how they improved them. Alternatively, students could be asked to work independently to annotate their improved responses by identifying and labelling the changes they made, with an explanation of why what they have done is an improvement.

Use the Checklist for success on slide 3 to reinforce the points that students should include for a higher-level response.

Plenary	Ask for three volunteers to read their reviews to the class. After each reading, other students should suggest one thing the student did well and one point for development. Make sure students are encouraging rather than disparaging, making suggestions in a positive way. They could call on the speaking and listening skills they have learned in earlier chapters.

Speaking in character

Learning objectives

7SL1; 7SL2; 7SL4

Differentiated learning outcomes

- **Lower: All students must** create a character's voice in role.
- **Mid: Most students should** use detail to develop a character's voice.
- **High: Some students could** create narrative and character using detail when in role.

Resources

- **Student Book**: pp. 136–137
- **Worksheet**: 5.7
- **PPT**: 5.7
- **Workbook links**: Unit 5.7, p. 72

Introducing the skills

Explain to students that role-play is when you perform a speech or dialogue in character. Imagining that you are a character from a story can help you understand their thoughts and feelings more clearly.

Briefly recap what students know about the characters of Cecily and Miss Peabody from Topic 5.2, and then read the extract on page 136 of the Student Book around the class.

Ask students to complete Question 1, jotting down a list of adjectives to describe how they might feel if they were Cecily. Take feedback and write up a list of adjectives on the board.

Give extra support by suggesting a few adjectives as starting points – for example, 'angry' or 'worried'.

Developing the skills

Students should complete Questions 2 and 3 independently, using the grids on Worksheet 5.7. When they have finished, ask students to share their ideas with a partner, who should give them feedback, identifying one point that is excellent and one point that could be developed further and improved upon.

Use the grids in PowerPoint 5.7 to take feedback from one pair and talk through it with the class.

Give extra challenge by asking students to extend the narrative by thinking about what Cecily plans to do after she has rescued her brother.

Applying the skills

Ask students to answer Question 4 on their own. They may want to make brief notes to help with their speech, but they should focus on the verbal aspects – in particular the tone of voice of their chosen character. When students have finished writing in the role as one character, they could extend the activity by preparing and giving a speech as the other.

Plenary	Select students to perform their speech to the class. Give constructive feedback on how well they captured the feelings of the character based on the earlier activities.

Cambridge Checkpoint English
Stage 7

Learning objectives
7Wa1; 7Wt1

Checkpoint progress test
* Paper 2, Section B

Differentiated learning outcomes
* **Lower: All students must** plan a story using a spider diagram.
* **Mid: Most students should** plan a story, dividing their ideas into characters, setting and plot.
* **High: Some students could** generate and shape their ideas in different ways and convey them clearly.

Resources
* **Student Book**: pp. 138–139
* **Worksheet**: 5.8
* **PPT**: 5.8
* **Workbook links**: Unit 5.8, p. 73

Introducing the skills

Ask students to work in pairs to answer Question 1, then take feedback from a couple of pairs. Show students slide 1 of PowerPoint 5.8, which gives advice for generating story ideas.

> **Give extra support** by explaining to students that they can use a list or a spider diagram to note down their thoughts. A spider diagram means they can put down lots of ideas, and then work on the order afterwards.
>
> **Give extra challenge** by encouraging students who have differing orders to explain and justify their choices.

Show students slide 2, then ask up to 10 students to come up with one word each that they think of when they see the word 'mysterious'. Students should then complete Question 2.

Developing the skills

Work through the information on page 139 of the Student Book, which discusses the categories used to help plan a story: plot, character and setting. Give students Worksheet 5.8 to help them work out what additional points they could add to their spider diagram. They should then complete Question 3 in pairs. Each pair should present a summary of their plans to another pair of students.

Applying the skills

Ask students to complete Question 4 in small groups. For each section of the task, students should deliver their ideas to their partner, then receive feedback. The first part asks for an overview, and students should aim to summarise what their story is about and who would find it interesting. This feeds into the next section, in which students should select three elements of their story to present. These could be plot, setting and characters, for example.

Plenary	Select students to deliver their presentations to the class. Ask other students to give two positive points and two points for development or improvement for each presentation.

Punctuating speech in narrative

Learning objectives

7Wp7

Checkpoint progress test

- Paper 2, Section B

Differentiated learning outcomes

- **Lower: All students must** use some punctuation in dialogue.
- **Mid: Most students should** use punctuation to show when different characters are speaking.
- **High: Some students could** use a range of punctuation marks to make it clear how characters feel.

Resources

- **Student Book**: pp. 140–141
- **Worksheet**: 5.9
- **PPT**: 5.9
- **Workbook links**: Unit 5.9, p. 74

Introducing the skills

Display slide 1 of PowerPoint 5.8, which lists some of the rules for punctuating speech. Then ask students to read the annotated text on page 140 of the Student Book, pausing at each of the annotations to make sure they have understood the feature being explained and the effect that it has.

Ask students to answer Questions 1 and 2 on their own. Take brief feedback. Then give students Worksheet 5.9 and ask them to answer the first two questions. In a class discussion, raise the idea that question marks can sometimes show a range of emotions and ask students to identify an example of this in the annotated extract.

Use the other activity on the worksheet to consolidate their understanding of the rules of punctuating speech.

Developing the skills

In groups of three, get students discuss both parts of Question 3:

- What are the feelings of the main characters in this extract?
- How do you know?

They should make notes during their discussion, and then use them to write up a paragraph on their own.

Give extra support by allowing students to break up their answer into separate sections with subheadings dealing with each character: Jimmy, Georgie and the younger man.

Applying the skills

Ask students to complete Question 4. When they have done so, display slide 2, which contains the unpunctuated text. Ask individual students to come up and put in the punctuation based on their own answers. If there are any mistakes, find out how many students made the same error and recap the rules as necessary.

Give extra challenge by asking students who finish quickly to continue the dialogue, using their own ideas of how the episode might unfold.

Plenary	At the end of the session, ask students to swap their paragraphs with a partner and use the 'Check your progress' points in the Student Book to peer-assess each other's work and give them an idea of which level they are working at.

Cambridge Checkpoint English
Stage 7

Learning objectives

7Wa8; 7Wt1; 7Wt2

Checkpoint progress test

- Paper 2, Section A

Differentiated learning outcomes

- **Lower: All students must** use connectives to show how events are linked.
- **Mid: Most students should** use long paragraphs to add detail and short paragraphs to present action.
- **High: Some students could** create characters using the first-person and third-person voice.

Resources

- **Student Book**: pp. 142–143
- **Worksheet**: 5.10
- **PPT**: 5.10
- **Workbook links**: Unit 5.10, p. 75

Introducing the skills

Display PowerPoint 5.10 and give students Worksheet 5.10. Talk about how there are connectives of time and connectives of order. Ask individual students to explain when each of the connectives in the word bank might be useful. As you go through each example on the slide, allocating it to a category, students should write the answers in the grid on the worksheet and keep it for reference for the writing activity at the end of the lesson.

Ask students to read the extract on page 142 of the Student Book and share their initial thoughts with a partner. Did they enjoy the passage? How did it make them feel?

Ask students to complete Questions 1 and 2 individually. The genre of the text is action, shown by the exciting verbs, and by the violent behaviour of the characters. For Question 2, students should have the following notes:

Paragraph 2: somebody tries to stab Jimmy: he moves just in time.
Paragraph 3: Jimmy sees two masked intruders; one shines a torch in his face. **Paragraph 4**: one asks about Jimmy's identity.
Paragraph 5: this question is answered positively.
Paragraph 6: one of the men raises his knife to attack Jimmy; he has no way to escape.

Developing the skills

Reinforce the fact that this extract is written in the third person (using 'he') describing a character (Jimmy). Some readers feel that the first person, using 'I' and 'me' is more exciting. What do students think? After a brief discussion, students should complete Questions 3 and 4.

Give extra support by encouraging students to highlight a copy of the passage every time the text says 'Jimmy'. They can then read the sentence aloud to work out if it makes more sense to put 'I' or 'me'.

Give extra challenge by asking students to note down the tone (the narrator's attitude) and the mood (how it makes the reader feel).

Applying the skills

Ask students to complete Question 5. When they have written a first draft, ask them to swap with a partner to 'workshop' their writing. The partner should comment (through annotation) on the use of paragraphs and connectives.

Learning objectives

7Wt1

Checkpoint progress test

* Paper 2, Section B

Differentiated learning outcomes

* **Lower: All students must** plan a story in response to the title.
* **Mid: Most students should** write a draft of a short story, following a plan and using a clear structure.
* **High: Some students could** use prompt questions and examples to improve their draft.

Resources

* **Student Book**: pp. 144–147
* **Worksheet**: 5.11
* **PPT**: 5.11
* **Workbook links**: Unit 5.11, pp. 76–77

Your task

Recap with students what information they should identify when reading task instructions – for example, the required form, content, purpose and audience. Once they are clear on these, they could spend a few minutes in pairs noting the implications of those requested in the task by making a checklist of features to include. The whole class could then work together to draw up a checklist to display while students attempt the task.

Explain to students that they will be writing a short story using suspense and mystery. The stimulus title is 'The Stolen Parcel'. Remind students that they will have to check back on and employ all the writing skills that they have built up in this chapter.

Approaching the task

Show slide 1 of PowerPoint 5.11. Select five students to come up and annotate ideas around the key words for Question 1 and to explain briefly to the class why they thought these were good ideas. They should use their ideas from this activity to build up their own plan in response to Question 2–4. Give students Worksheet 5.11 and ask them to use the blank spider diagram as their starting point. Remind them to use lines and arrows to show how ideas are connected. They could also use numbers to sequence plot points.

Once they have completed the spider diagram, remind students of the grid they completed in Topic 5.8. They should use a similar structure to complete Question 5. After students have completed the grid, ask them to swap with a partner. They should read their partner's grid to see if they can imagine the progress of the story and anticipate any confusion.

Students should then complete Question 6. As an extension activity, they could draw out storyboards of their stories and their partner's. They should then give the partner's storyboard back for comparison. Any differences will indicate points of confusion that need to be discussed and resolved before writing.

Ask students to complete Question 7, making frequent reference to their planning. This could be set as a homework task to connect the different stages of planning and writing. Otherwise, students will require independent working time to complete this. Encourage students to read through their drafts at least once before sharing them.

If this is taking place in a lesson, students may want to swap their work with a partner so that they can workshop each other's pieces, using the sections of Question 8 for guidance. If the work is taking place independently, encourage the use of colour-coding. Students should use a different colour pen for each of the six requirements in Question 8. Every time that they have addressed one they should underline or highlight in the relevant colour. The finished document will give a quick and clear visual map of how many of the requirements they have addressed, and how often.

Reflecting on your progress

This section of the topic could be used *before* students write their own piece to help them gain a thorough understanding of how they will be assessed and how to improve their writing. They can use the response examples as models for assessing their own work and can refer back to previous topics to consolidate their understanding. They can peer-check each other's evaluations before writing the improved versions. Afterwards, you can check both 'before' and 'after' versions to monitor their understanding and progress.

Alternatively, this section can be used *after* they have written and assessed their short stories. You can then help them focus on the learning through the most relevant example, response and comments, as well as your own assessment of their work. After completing Questions 9 and 10, students can produce an improved version of their own article to self-assess using the 'Checklist for success' on slide 2 in PowerPoint 5.11.

Display slide 3 in PowerPoint 5.11, which shows the summary progress points from the end of the chapter. Students should use these points to self-assess their learning and in particular to identify these points in the improved story they have completed for this topic.

Learning objectives

7Rv1; 7Rv2; 7Rv4; 7Wa4; 7Wa8

Checkpoint progress test

- Paper 1, Section A

Differentiated learning outcomes

- **Lower: All students must** write a paragraph that uses evidence from a text.
- **Mid: Most students should** use speech marks for quotations in a paragraph of analysis.
- **High: Some students could** select the most suitable evidence and write a paragraph with accurate punctuation.

Resources

- **Student Book**: pp. 150–153
- **Worksheet**: 6.1
- **PPT**: 6.1
- **Workbook links**: Unit 6.1, pp. 78–79

Introducing the skills

Chapter 6 focuses on literary analysis. While this is not a requirement of the Cambridge Secondary 1 English curriculum framework or assessments, it nevertheless has the benefit both of broadening the range of material students encounter and beginning to embed skills at a basic level, which will be useful in literature studies.

Ask students to talk for two minutes about any dramatic or theatrical performances they have seen. These might be at school, in the local community or professional productions in big towns or cities. Listen to a small number of students commenting on what they remember about the productions. Then ask the class how people know whether it is worth going to see a particular play, dance or musical performance.

Elicit from the discussion the idea that people read reviews – in their literal meaning, a 're-seeing' (looking back over a performance). Ask students where they think such reviews are found. Who writes them? Have any students reviewed a theatrical performance for the school newspaper, for example?

Read aloud Lia's review of 'Beauty and the Beast' on page 150 of the Student Book. Work with students to draw out the meaning of some of the more challenging vocabulary – 'magnificent', 'shimmering', 'fragile' – to help when they come to analyse the text later in the topic.

Ask students to work on their own to answer Questions 1 and 2, then take brief feedback: the play was 'Beauty and the Beast' (mentioned in the first sentence) and Lia 'loved it'.

Students should then work in pairs on Question 3. Share responses: they should understand that they were able to determine Lia's overall view because of the words and phrases she chose to describe elements of the play, for example, 'magnificent', 'loved every minute', 'production worked well', 'wonderful'.

Give extra challenge by asking some students what words or phrases Lia could have used if she did not like the production. You could introduce the idea of antonyms here – words that are opposite in meaning (wonderful/dreadful, loved/hated, and so on). Make sure students understand that antonyms should be the same type of word (adjective, verb etc.).

Developing the skills

For Question 4, distribute Worksheet 6.1 and explain that the students' task here is to decide what Lia's focus is in each paragraph of the review. Emphasise that a good analysis (which is what a review is) will examine particular elements of a text, play, film, etc., so that the reader gets an overall impression of what the reviewer thinks, as well as understanding the detail about individual likes and dislikes.

When students have completed their grids, take feedback on what they think Lia thought in paragraphs 3–5, and talk about the evidence they have chosen to back up their thoughts.

Cambridge Checkpoint English
Stage 7

Draw students' attention to the fact that the examples given in the 'Evidence' column are in speech marks and are quotations from the review. Have students followed the same rules when choosing their own evidence? Get them to double-check. Explain that this is necessary for a reader to understand that the words are Lia's, not their own.

Now ask students to work on their own on Questions 5 and 6, before taking feedback from the class as a whole. Clearly Student B gives evidence in the form of quotations. Make sure that all students are able to point to the words *inside the speech marks*, which are the ones that show direct evidence.

For Question 6, option c is the correct response. Check that all students have written out the whole paragraph, including the final quotation correctly.

Use PowerPoint 6.1 to sum up the rules for adding evidence in an analysis and to show how a paragraph including a quotation as evidence should look. Display this after students have completed Question 6, so they can check to see they have written their analysis paragraph accurately.

Applying the skills

Before completing Question 7, make sure that all students look again at the row in their grid that deals with paragraph 3. Confirm that they are clear about Lia's thoughts and the evidence they will use. Then ask them to write their paragraph.

When they have completed their paragraph, go over the 'Checklist for success' to remind them that they should have put any evidence inside speech marks and summed up Lia's thoughts in that paragraph. Students can revise their analysis if they need to.

Give extra support by showing students the following prompts to help complete their paragraph:

- *Lia thought that the set design as a whole was…*
- *She particularly admired the staircase, which was…*
- *She said the design of it was very…*
- *Because…*

Plenary	When students have completed their paragraph, go over the 'Checklist for success' to remind them that they should have put any evidence inside speech marks and summed up Lia's thoughts in that paragraph. You might wish to suggest that students revise their analysis for homework if they need to.

Learning objectives
7Rv1 and 7Rv4

Checkpoint progress test
- Paper 2, Section A

Differentiated learning outcomes
- **Lower: All students must** write at least two lines of script.
- **Mid: Most students should** write a complete section of script.
- **High: Some students could** develop a longer scene or act of script.

Resources
- **Student Book**: pp. 154–157
- **Worksheet**: 6.2
- **PPT**: 6.2
- **Workbook links**: Unit 6.2, pp. 80–81

Introducing the skills

Ask students to work in groups of three or four to discuss Question 1. You could encourage them to think about a myth, legend or well-known folk tale from their own culture but if they struggle to do so, offer suggestions such as 'Cinderella' or 'Anansi the Spider'.

Ask each group to feed back on one story they discussed. Explore the different versions of it. Is there a 'correct' version, or are there many versions that are all slightly different from one another? Elicit the idea that the story might have been spoken aloud originally before someone wrote it down, which is why several versions of traditional tales often exist. You could play a version of the game 'Chinese whispers', with a made-up story, to show how easily a spoken tale can change.

Read Text A aloud, then select three students to read Text B to the class. One should read the non-speaking sections and the other two should take the parts of the Beast's Man and the Father.

For Question 2, ask students to jot down their own answers and then share them with a friend before feeding back to the class as a whole. The tale is 'Beauty and the Beast'. The characters are similar, but not identical: the story has Beauty, her father and the Beast; the play has Beauty, her father and the Beast's servant (Beast's Man). Students should recognise that Text B comes from a play because it identifies clearly who should speak by putting their names on the left. There are also other clues, such as the use of the word 'Act'. The main difference is that we are told what Beauty is thinking in the story (and it is told in the first person, 'I'), but in a play feelings must be *shown* rather than described.

Ask students to complete Question 3 on their own as you read each option. Then, in pairs, they should complete the grid in Question 4.

- Play features are c), e), g), h) and i).
- Story features are a), b), c), d) and f).

Give extra challenge by asking students to discuss the advantages and disadvantages of the two ways of telling the same story. They could consider the fact that a written play is meant to be shared as a performance, while a story (unless read aloud) is for reading alone.

Developing the skills

Read aloud Question 5 to the students and ask them to decide which of the three options is correct. The answer is a). The gesture of putting his arms around his daughter demonstrates the father's care for her.

Move on to Questions 6 and 7. Students should be able to answer these on their own, but make sure they have fully understood the conventions of play scripts before they do so. If necessary, use the two slides in PowerPoint 6.2 to summarise the conventions and show students an example of a correct play-script layout. The answers are:

Cambridge Checkpoint English
Stage 7

6 Version A is correct.

7 Version B is incorrect because it has past tense verbs and speech marks.
Version C is incorrect because, although it uses the present tense correctly, it still has speech marks.

Applying the skills

Read aloud the second extract from 'Beauty and the Beast'. To help students prepare for Questions 8 and 9, give them Worksheet 6.2 and ask them to mark up the extract as indicated in the instructions. They should be looking for:

- verbs they might be able to use in the script (these should be turned into present tense forms)

- speech marks that should be removed

- other text that they cannot use in a script (students will need to think about how they can get the same ideas across in script form)

- any other changes, such as where characters' names should go.

Students should then complete Question 8. Tell them to copy out the start of the play script on page 157 of the Student Book and then continue the script themselves. They should be allowed to refer back to the correct layout of play scripts as they write.

Question 9 requires students to explain the decisions they have made using sticky notes or annotations. Individual students could explain their work to groups or to the rest of the class.

Give extra support by working in a guided group with less confident students. Help them work together to compose the next line of the script. For example:

The BEAST enters, quietly.
BEAST (*tenderly*): What is it?

Draw out the changes that have been made and what has been left out. Then ask the group to work in pairs to turn the remaining lines into script. Afterwards, they could share and review each other's work.

Plenary	Finish by asking students to close any books they have and quickly work in pairs to note down the key features/conventions of plays. Share these as a whole class, embedding their knowledge of those features. You could suggest that they continue the script for homework, writing a new scene to follow the one they have just transposed.

Discussing key ideas from a text

Learning objectives
7R02; 7Rx1; 7Rv3; 7SL1; 7SL2; 7SL5; 7SL6; 7SL7

Checkpoint progress test
- Paper 1, Section A

Differentiated learning outcomes
- **Lower: All students must** contribute to a discussion and stick to the set task.
- **Mid: Most students should** give opinions in a polite way and support them with reasons.
- **High: Some students could** give opinions and support them, as well as listening to and encouraging others in the group.

Resources
- **Student Book**: pp. 158–161
- **Worksheets**: 6.3a and 6.3b
- **PPT**: 6.3
- **Workbook links**: Unit 6.3, pp. 82–83

Introducing the skills

Introduce the idea that everyone is an individual when it comes to speaking. We all use a different tone of voice and facial expressions; we have phrases that we use frequently and particular ways that we speak in certain situations. Some people are quieter members of a group of friends; others dominate and speak up. Ask students to talk with a partner for a few minutes about what sort of speaker they are, using the prompt questions from the introductory paragraph in the Student Book.

Move the focus on the tale of Cinderella and ask small groups to discuss the plot .Feed back to the class – did everyone agree on the story, or were there different versions? Explain that they are going to read about the history of the story, and their discussions about it will help them improve their speaking and listening skills.

Read aloud the history of 'Cinderella' as a story, pausing for any difficult vocabulary. (You may need to explain words such as 'miraculously', 'pumpkin', 'footmen.')

When you have read the text, ask students to use their scanning skills to find the key points in part a) of Question 1. Look for the word 'version' and a synonym for 'well-known' ('famous'). The answer is Charles Perrault's.

For part b), students need to read across the text. They may find it useful to compile a grid to compare versions. The main elements are: Cinderella's poverty and mistreatment; being transformed or given nice clothes for an event (not always a ball); and the slipper that is left behind. For part c) they should note that there are over 300 versions of the story.

Students should then work alone to jot down some ideas in answer to Question 2.

Developing the skills

Students should read the 'conversation' on page 160. They could do this by themselves or four students could take parts and read it for the class. After the reading, ask students if they think this was a good discussion. Why, or why not?

Students should work in pairs to answer Questions 3–5, then join with another pair and compare their answers. Suggested responses are:

3 **a)** Sia; **b)** Levi (talks about Disney); **c)** Jay

4 Daz appears to be the most polite and sensible.

5 Sia could have disagreed in a more pleasant way, giving reasons such as 'Not all girls expect to marry princes'. Levi could have talked about aspects of the story such as family arguments or dreams for the future. Jay could have supported Daz by keeping the group on track.

Use PowerPoint 6.3 to expand on the key points in the bullet list at the top of page 161. As you show each of the three slides, ask students to think about which of these skills they most need to focus on for their own development as speakers or listeners. They should make notes if necessary to use as prompts in their later discussions.

Cambridge Checkpoint English
Stage 7

For Question 6, students should work in groups to discuss Question 2. They should each be able to refer to the notes they made when addressing Question 2. Before they begin, give students a copy of Worksheet 6.3a and ask them to use the grid on it to keep track of how well their discussion follows the rules. One member of the group should act as an observer or evaluator and tick off boxes each time a member of the group does something well. Alternatively, you could use the grid yourself to evaluate group performances.

Give extra challenge by asking one student to play a 'bad' speaker who interrupts and does a lot of things wrong. They should perform this part secretly, without other members of the group knowing. See how other students deal with the bad speaker. Will the student assessing the discussion notice?

Applying the skills

For Question 7, you could play the role of the famous director Simon Spielbug to make the task fun. Read the note out (in an American accent, perhaps!). Then give groups a maximum of 10 minutes to have their discussion. Before they begin, explain that at least one person in the group will be expected to present the group's ideas to the class at the end. Ideas must be based on a successful, co-operative discussion, with all students taking part.

After their discussions, each group should present their ideas. Hold a vote for the class to choose their favourite ideas overall.

Finally, give out copies of Worksheet 6.3b and ask students to self-assess their own performance in the group task.

Give extra support by taking on the role of chairperson in a group and guiding students through the discussion. Some students may be too shy to contribute, so encourage them to take part and suggest ideas. If it helps, these students could talk in pairs first within the group to build their confidence.

Plenary	Finish by asking students to close their books and, as a class, name the key features of an effective and productive discussion. The answers are on page 161 of the Student Book. You might want to probe a little deeper to check individuals actually know what each point means in practice – for example, what does it mean to 'encourage others to speak'? Can they give examples of what a group member might actually say?

Learning objectives

7Rw3; 7Rw8; 7Rv3; 7Rv4

Checkpoint progress test

- Paper 2, Section A

Differentiated learning outcomes

- **Lower: All students must** identify what a verse is and basic rhymes.
- **Mid: Most students should** comment on patterns, verses and sounds in poems.
- **High: Some students could** comment on the effects of a poet's choices of structures and sounds.

Resources

- **Student Book**: pp. 162–165
- **Worksheet**: 6.4
- **PPT**: 6.4
- **Workbook links**: Unit 6.4, pp. 84–85

Introducing the skills

Ask students to look at the picture of the door on page 162 of the Student Book for one or two minutes. They should then answer Question 1 in discussion with a partner. Take brief feedback. Students may have noted that the door looks quite grand but it is also dark and rather grim – it does not necessarily appear welcoming.

Give extra support by allowing some students to write their ideas around a copy of the photo on a large sheet of paper, encouraging them to write down whatever comes to mind.

Read aloud the text on 'The gothic' and ask students to work in pairs to respond to Questions 2 and 3. To answer part a) of Question 2, they will need to look for information related to 'plot' (or a similar word, 'story'). Point out that there is another question related to character, so to avoid that detail at the moment. Possible answers for Question 2 are as follows:

- **a)** Plot: mystery, suspense and danger; revenge, disappearance, murder, people turning from good to evil; the supernatural
- **b)** People: cruel older villains; orphans, girls in danger
- **c)** Settings: frightening places such as castles, mansions, ruins in mountains or forests
- **d)** Stories: *Dracula*, *The Mysteries of Udolpho*, *The Castle of Otranto*

When students have answered Question 3, take some feedback from pairs and ask individuals what is gothic about the examples they have chosen.

Give students Worksheet 6.4, which has a copy of the poem on it. Students should use this to match the gothic features (on the right) to the poem while they are reading it.

Now ask students to work on their own to answer Questions 4 and 5. They should share answers with a partner before reporting back to the class as a whole, or to small groups. Possible responses might be:

- **4 a)** In the first verse, he describes the setting of the castle (the 'green woods'). Then in the second verse, he mentions them again before saying what they contain.
- **b)** The phrase 'white castle' is repeated, as is 'black mountain'.
- **c)** The second and fourth lines rhyme in each verse.
- **5** Options a) and b) could be correct. The structure allows the poet to start with the mountains, zoom into the woods, through the door and into the castle. However, it also allows him to end with the 'close-up' on the Prince, which creates mystery.

Give extra challenge by asking students to create their own video with music to represent the poem. They do not need to use moving images, but could select appropriate photos from the internet and add lines from the poem over the image in their video. They could even record themselves reading the poem aloud. Students should be able to explain why each image has been selected.

Cambridge Checkpoint English
Stage 7

Developing the skills

Students should work on their own to answer Questions 6, 8 and 9. Once they have done so, take general feedback. For example:

6 They all have 'perfect' rhymes except the first – 'broods' (pronounced 'brudes') and 'woods' (usually pronounced like 'woulds').

8 Ballads often use rhymes because they are linked to songs – words that were spoken or sung aloud, so needed to be memorised. Rhymes help the brain remember the pattern.

9 The four words are 'sighs', 'soft', 'moans' and 'groans'.

Question 7 is a longer task, so may need to be set as a separate task in class or for homework.

For Questions 10 and 11, students can work in pairs to discuss the mysteries:

- Why is she an 'old' princess?
- What made her a 'ghost'?
- Is the prince a 'ghost' too?
- How are they related? Brother and sister, or something else?
- How is it that the prince who is 'dead' seems to be alive?
- Who poisoned him and why?

Applying the skills

Before students attempt Question 12, go over the task carefully with them, reminding them that they have covered all these areas during the lesson.

Use PowerPoint 6.4 to model the process for completing the task. You may wish to print these slides out for students to use as a template. Remind them to use quotations in the way they learned about earlier in this chapter.

More confident students may wish to expand the three paragraphs by adding further details of their own.

Plenary	Check with students that they are clear what is meant by 'structure' in relation to texts: it is the form, shape and the way in which the text is divided both visually and in terms of content and order of ideas.

Learning objectives
7R01; 7Rw3; 7Rv1

Checkpoint progress test
- Paper 2, Section A

Differentiated learning outcomes
- **Lower: All students must** recognise how connectives and quotations are used together.
- **Mid: Most students should** choose connectives and quotations and use them in a paragraph.
- **High: Some students could** select the most appropriate connectives and quotes, and use them thoughtfully.

Resources
- **Student Book**: pp. 166–167
- **Worksheet**: 6.5
- **PPT**: 6.5
- **Workbook links**: Unit 6.5, p. 86

Introducing the skills

Explain that this unit refers to the poem 'In a Far Land' from Topic 6.4. Provide students with copies of the poem if necessary. Remind students that it is important to be precise when selecting information from texts for analysis, and when quoting particular words or phrases.

Display slide 1 from PowerPoint 6.5 and ask students to work in pairs to answer Questions 1–3 in the Student Book. Take brief feedback. Use the slide to demonstrate that by being precise, the student is able to make absolutely clear the selection of relevant evidence.

Developing the skills

Display slide 2, which shows the new paragraph. Ask students to work on their own to complete Questions 4–6. Take brief feedback from individuals. (The answers are 'second', 'first', 'the green woods'.) You could get students to come up to the board and point out / explain the specific selection.

Write or display the paragraph in Question 7 on a screen or large sheet of paper so students can try out different connectives. Cut out the cards on Worksheet 6.5. Mix them up and ask students to select appropriate connective words that best fit at the start of the second sentence. 'In contrast', 'However' and 'Yet' all work. 'But' is usually best avoided at the start of a sentence.

Applying the skills

Students should complete Question 8 on their own. As they work, ask individuals to explain the function of the words or phrases they are using (e.g. to show sequence, create a link between ideas, indicate difference or contrast).

Plenary	Ask students to explain what they have learned about the sorts of words and phrases that help with precision.

Cambridge Checkpoint English
Stage 7

Learning objectives
7Rv3

Checkpoint progress test
* Paper 1, Section A

Differentiated learning outcomes

* **Lower: All students must** comment on the similarities between two poems.
* **Mid: Most students should** comment on how two poems are alike and different in terms of structure.
* **High: Some students could** analyse in precise detail the forms and structures of two poems.

Resources

* **Student Book**: pp. 168–171
* **Worksheet**: 6.6
* **PPT**: 6.6
* **Workbook links**: Unit 6.6, pp. 87–88

Your task

Explain to students that they will be looking at two poems dealing with similar subject matter. They need to identify the similarities and differences between the two poems. One of the poems draws on the fairy tale 'Jack and the Beanstalk'. Students may be familiar with it, but if not you could provide a more detailed account than the one in the Student Book.

Read the task aloud, making sure all students are aware of what it requires. Then read the two poems to the class. Point out the difficulties of reading the second poem aloud, but identify the line that makes sense: 'But overnight the tiny seeds grew and grew and grew and grew into a huge beanstalk which Jack climbed quickly up till he reached the top.'

Approaching the task

Worksheet 6.6. contains copies of both poems so that students can make notes around the text according to the features in the table on page 169 of the Student Book:

* **Story/plot:** what is happening and to whom
* **Structure and layout:** rhyme, order or sequence of words, phrases, lines, repetitions, sound effects, number of verses, etc.
* **Language choices:** vocabulary, imagery, description, tenses, etc.

You should elicit the following:

'The Magic Seeds'	'Jack and the Beanstalk, Part 2'
The story is very simple and is about an 'old woman' who plants a seed and from it grows a tree with a bird that attracts everyone to it. There is no obvious 'message' to the poem except in nature's ability to create beauty. In fact you could say that all seeds are 'magic' as they create something from nothing.	The story is very simple – Jack climbs a beanstalk!
There is regular rhythm and pattern to the lines, like a child's rhyme. There are regular rhymed couplets ('seed'/'weed', 'bed'/'red', etc.) and each idea in each line seems to lead on to the one in the next, so that the corn seed creates the yellow weed.	This is a shape poem in which the shape of the text represents what is being described. The words grow, like the beanstalk in the first line; then the words that describe Jack's ascent are placed either side of the trunk of the beanstalk, like Jack's legs or feet climbing up it.
The language is very simple – a lot of use of colour, with the white bird perhaps being symbolic of peace/love?	There is no obvious message, but the shape of the poem could be said to be 'magic' in that it grows in front of our eyes – we follow Jack up the beanstalk as we read it.

Give extra challenge by asking students to create their own first verse for 'Jack and the Beanstalk'. They may need to research the story (how he is sent to market to sell the family cow but exchanges it for magic beans). Or they could deal with the section where Jack's mother throws the beans out of the window in anger.

Students should then complete Question 1, following the structure provided in the Student Book – a paragraph on each poem, then a final third paragraph comparing the two poems. Students can write more if they wish.

Give extra support by providing a writing frame. For example:

- *In the first poem, we find out how...*
- *The structure of the poem is...*
- *The effect of this is...*

Reflecting on your progress

Read Response 1 and the comments that follow it. Use slides 1 and 2 of PowerPoint 6.6 to explore how the first response could be improved. Slide 1 shows the first response and slide 2 an improved version. The key things to draw out are the *precision* – an essential part of analysis skills – and the need to explain *effects* when quoting from a text.

Move on to Response 2. Read it and ask students how it could be improved.

Use slides 3 and 4 to explore how the second response could be improved. Slide 3 shows the response and slide 4 an improved version. Draw out the importance of developing ideas and taking them a step further when analysing specific words, phrases or lines.

Show students the final slide, containing the 'Checklist for success', and ask them to assess their own (or a partner's) work against the points.

Plenary	Complete the work by asking students to identify the key skills and techniques they now feel they have mastered, and to identify one or two particular areas for improvement. This can be recorded and used as a measure for improvement in future tasks that address similar objectives or content.

Learning objectives

7Rx1; 7Rx2; 7Ri1; 7Rw2; 7W01; 7W02; 7Wa1; 7Wa2; 7Wa3; 7Wa4; 7Wa5; 7Wa6; 7Wa7; 7Wa8; 7Wa9; 7Wt1; 7Wt2; 7Wp1; 7Wp2; 7Wp3; 7Wp4; 7Wp5; 7Wp6; 7Wp7; 7Ws1

Differentiated learning outcomes

- **Lower: Some students could** use the guidance to self-assess and improve their work.
- **Mid: Most students should** use the guidance to become fairly confident in their use of time and in fulfilling the requirements of the individual tasks.
- **High: Some students could** use the advice to become familiar with the demands of working under exam-type conditions and with rigorous assessment criteria.

Resources

- **Student Book**: pp. 174–177
- **Worksheets**: 7.1a–e
- **PPT**: 7.1
- **Workbook links**: Unit 7.1, pp. 89–90

Introducing the skills

Remind students that Task 1 is based on non-fiction. Ask them which reading skills they might use more of in this task compared with Task 3, which is based on fiction. Clarify that *inference* is of less importance this time and that questions about language use are likely to feature more techniques related to persuasion and clarifying ideas and viewpoint.

Use PowerPoint 7.1 to take students through the type of questions they can expect in an assessment context and how to answer them.

Explain that there are six common types of question. As they work through the questions, students could annotate them to indicate their type (1–6). You may wish to ask students to make posters of the various examples and acronyms that are shown on the slides.

The acronym LEHR is used to explain an easy technique for answering a 'Why' question relating to a writer's choice of language:

L = **link** to the question
E = state the **effect** created
H = explain **how** the technique creates that effect
R = describe what this helps the **reader** understand about more general things (characters, feelings, atmosphere in the whole text)

A model is given on slides 7 and 8. You could show students these slides again when they are about to tackle this type of question, to remind them of this technique.

Give extra support by allowing students to use Chapters 1, 2 and 3 from the Student Book while answering the questions in Task 1.

Developing the skills

Ask students to read the tips on Worksheet 7.1a or read them aloud with the students. They could also be the focus of a homework activity, in which students turn these tips into a self-help leaflet or set of posters for the classroom.

Give extra challenge by asking some students to create their own questions for each question type explored in the top tips, using a passage from earlier in the Student Book.

Give students Worksheet 7.1b, which contains a set of icons relating to different types of question. Working in pairs, ask students to annotate the Questions in Tasks 1 and 2, placing the appropriate icon at the side of each question. A copy of the questions can be found on Worksheets 7.1c and 7.1d.

Alternatively, students could come up with their own set of icons for each of the points.

Applying the skills

Students should complete Tasks 1 and 2 independently. However, at this stage you may wish to break down the experience to make it less formidable. To do so, use the following steps:

1 Allow students five minutes to read the first passage in Task 1. Discuss the various strategies that they might use to tackle words that they are not familiar with.

2 Remind students to use the icons they have drawn on the worksheet to guide them. Then give them 20 minutes to answer the first 10 questions.

3 If continuing with the rest of Task 1, allow students five minutes to read the second extract. Then give them 40 minutes to answer the next seven questions.

4 Read Task 2 out loud to the class and emphasise the importance of planning.

5 Allow 60 minutes for students to complete the writing task. Students should use Worksheet 7.1e to help them with their planning.

Note that these timings do not reflect the sort of timings likely in a formal examination context, but are designed to ease students gently into this scenario.

At this point, you may decide to ask students to assess their work on Unit 7.1 before moving to the next assessment in 7.2. In this case, you could use Lesson Plan 7.3, as it will lead you through the self-assessment process.

Give extra support by offering some students the questions one at a time. You could also offer support by time bonding their work time for them – dividing the amount of time that they would have in an assessment to ensure that they spend a proportionate amount of time on each question and do not waste time on questions where only 1 mark is available. This would mean approximately two minutes per mark available in Questions 1–17 (i.e. 10 minutes for a 5-mark question).

Learning objectives

7Ri1; 7Rw1; 7Rw2; 7W01; 7W02; 7Wa1; 7Wa2; 7Wa3; 7Wa4;
7Wa5; 7Wa6; 7Wa7; 7Wa8; 7Wa9; 7Wt1; 7Wt2; 7Wp1; 7Wp2;
7Wp3; 7Wp4; 7Wp5; 7Wp6; 7Wp7; 7Ws1

Differentiated learning outcomes

- **Lower: Some students could** use the guidance to self-assess and improve their work.
- **Mid: Most students should** use the guidance to become fairly confident in their use of time and in fulfilling the requirements of the individual tasks.
- **High: Some students could** use the advice to become familiar with the demands of working under exam-type conditions and with rigorous assessment criteria.

Resources

- **Student Book**: pp. 178–181
- **Worksheets**: 7.2a and 7.2b
- **PPT**: 7.2
- **Workbook links**: Unit 7.2, pp. 91–92

Introducing the skills

Remind students that Task 3 is based on fiction. Ask them which reading skills they might use more of in this task compared with Task 1, which was based on non-fiction. Clarify that *inference* is of more importance this time and that questions about language use will be likely to feature more *imagery* and different language techniques.

Use PowerPoint 7.2 to take students through the type of questions about language that they can expect in an assessment context. You may wish to ask students to make posters of the various examples and acronyms shown.

Draw attention to the fact that there is a 'new' question type featured here (Type 5) which asks students to use inference. This is often framed as a 'How is X feeling' or 'What is X's attitude' question. Slide 8 explains the new acronym, which is LEHR with the addition of a quote, Q, between the L and E, so the acronym is LQEHR. In this type of question, students are expected to select their own evidence to show that they know how an inferred idea has been suggested by the writer.

> **Give extra support** by allowing students to use Chapters 4 and 5 from the Student Book while answering the questions in Task 3.
>
> **Give extra challenge** by asking students to work in a group to create their own mini-exam, in which they predict the type of questions set and have a go at writing them.

Developing the skills

Ask students if they can remember the tips they used when preparing for Tasks 1 and 2. Brainstorm these and display them on the board so that students can see them.

Give out a copy of Tasks 3 and 4 on Worksheets 7.2a and 7.2b and ask students to use the icons that they designed (or used from Worksheet 7.1b) to independently annotate each question.

When tackling Tasks 1 and 2 this was a paired task, so there is an element of development here. Alternatively, students could continue to work in pairs or small groups on this activity. Once again, you may wish to consider dividing this task into two activities with students completing Task 3 in full before annotating Task 4.

If they have already completed the self-assessment activities for Tasks 1 and 2 (contained in Topic 7.3) then students may be ready to consider a more personal preparation for the tasks. You could ask them to consider their own self-evaluations from Worksheet 7.3c and set themselves some targets for improvement this time.

They can use the headings:

- Questions I did best on
- Questions I struggled with
- Strategies I need to use more

Applying the skills

Students should now complete Tasks 3 and 4 independently. However, at this stage you may wish to break down the experience to make it less formidable. To do so, use the following steps:

1 Allow students five minutes to read the first passage in Task 3. Discuss the various strategies that they might use to tackle words that they are not familiar with.

2 Remind students to use the icons they have drawn on the worksheet to guide them. Then give them 40 minutes to answer the questions.

3 Read Task 4 out loud to the class and emphasise the importance of planning.

4 Allow 60 minutes for Task 4. Students should use Worksheet 7.1e to aid with their planning. Again, if they have already completed Topic 7.3 then they may be able to identify areas of weakness in their planning and focus their energies on a specific area.

Note that these timings do not reflect the sort of timings likely in a formal examination context, but are designed to ease students gently into this scenario.

Give extra support by offering some students the questions one at a time. You could also offer support by time bonding their work time for them – dividing the amount of time that they would have in an assessment to ensure that they spend a proportionate amount of time on each question and do not waste time on questions where only 1 mark is available. This would mean approximately two minutes per mark available in Questions 1–12 (i.e. 10 minutes for a 5-mark question).

Learning objectives

Students will learn how to:

- approach examination-type tasks
- reflect on their performance in an examination-type task
- apply strategies to improve their performance on an examination-type task.

Differentiated learning outcomes

- **Lower: Some students could** use the guidance to self-assess and improve their work.
- **Mid: Most students should** use the guidance to become fairly confident in their use of time and in fulfilling the requirements of the individual tasks.
- **High: Some students could** use the advice to become familiar with the demands of working under exam-type conditions and with rigorous assessment criteria.

Resources

- **Student Book**: pp. 182–189
- **Worksheets**: 7.3a–c
- **PPT**: 7.3
- **Workbook links**: Unit 7.3, pp. 93–96

Introducing the skills

Once students have completed the questions for Tasks 1 and 2, Topic 7.3 offers a review of the questions with the answers and hints about areas where mistakes can be made. The worksheets associated with this topic contain a number of activities to encourage students to assess their own work. These can be used together at the end of all the non-fiction practice questions or separately after each task.

Using pages 182–188 of the Student Book, students should work in pairs to mark one of their sets of answers. Guide them through this process, one question at a time, reading the instructions and clarifying any 'examiner speak' such as: '1 mark for any reasonable explanation'. Explain that this means there is not an exact answer that is required. If a student has thought their answer through and has evidence for it, then that would be acceptable. Circulate around the room and clarify queries as students work through each question one at a time.

Developing the skills

As students mark each question, use the advice and hints to explore alternative answers and why they are not correct. Use PowerPoint 7.3 to highlight the key learning point for each question, with reference to examination technique.

Give students Worksheet 7.3a, which offers three sample responses to Question 15. Ask students to rank them in order of effectiveness and then use the grid on page 187 of the Student Book to mark them.

When they have completed this task, review their answers:

- Suggest that answer A is too short and does not cover the range of points. This would be lucky to get even one mark.
- Answer B is better, but the language is rather informal. It might be awarded 4 marks.
- Response C is the best and would gain 5 marks.

Next give out Worksheet 7.3b, which contains a sample response to Task 2, with annotations.

Ask students to decide which level this response is working at based on the left-hand column of the grid on page 189 of the Student Book.

Student should then repeat this process for the right-hand column by testing the order of the paragraphs in the article against those in the grid and deciding which descriptor fits it the best.

You should point out at this stage that in a more formal assessment situation the students' spelling, grammar, sentence structure and punctuation would also be assessed but that you will do this later.

> **Give extra challenge** by asking students to improve on the answer given on Worksheet 7.3b. They should try to add:
>
> * more descriptive details
> * more imagery.

Applying the skills

Ask students to mark the other set of answers in their pairs. This time they should give feedback about where the student whose work is being marked went wrong and what could be done to improve it.

Once students' responses have been reliably marked, hand out Worksheet 7.3c and ask students to conduct a self-review, looking at their own strengths and weaknesses by self-assessing and using the rankings to place themselves into a category for their performance. From this they should be able to identify their weakest areas and identify target question types for improvement.

Students could then look back to the skills icons against those questions (completed in Topic 5.1) and make a list of revisions that they want to make and sections of the book that they should revisit.

Learning objectives

Students will learn how to:

- approach examination-type tasks
- reflect on their performance in an examination-type task
- apply strategies to improve their performance on an examination-type task.

Differentiated learning outcomes

- **Lower: Some students could** use the guidance to self-assess and improve their work.
- **Mid: Most students should** use the guidance to become fairly confident in their use of time and in fulfilling the requirements of the individual tasks.
- **High: Some students could** use the advice to become familiar with the demands of working under exam-type conditions and with rigorous assessment criteria.

Resources

- **Student Book**: pp. 190–195
- **Worksheets**: 7.4a–c
- **PPT**: 7.4

Introducing the skills

Once students have completed the questions for Tasks 3 and 4, Topic 7.4 offers a review of the questions, with answers and hints about areas where mistakes can be made. The worksheets associated with this topic contain a number of activities to encourage students to assess their own work. These can be used together at the end of all the fiction practice questions, or separately after each task.

Using pages 190–195 of the Student Book, students should assess their own work. This represents a development from Topic 7.3, where students worked in pairs. However, some students may not yet be ready for this and you may prefer to arrange some in pairs or small groups.

Developing the skills

Circulate around the room and clarify individual student's queries as they work through each question one at a time. After they have marked each question, suggest that they look through the same pages, this time focusing on the alternative answers that may have been given and why they are not correct.

Give extra support by using PowerPoint 7.4 to highlight the key learning points with reference to examination technique.

Give extra challenge by asking students to create a PowerPoint similar to this, in which they identify the key learning points relating to each question.

When all students have self-assessed their work, hand out Worksheet 7.4a to get students thinking about the assessment process for some key questions. This shows two sample responses each for Questions 3 and 8. Get students to complete the Worksheet and then grade the answers. (For Question 3, A is 2 marks and B is 4 marks; for Question 8, A is 2 marks and B is 1 mark.)

Alternatively, this activity could be used as a targeted intervention for students who did not do well on these two questions, or as a paired activity with one student who did well on it in the assessment paired with one who did not do well.

Next use Worksheet 7.4b, which gives three sample responses to Question 12 and asks students to rank them. Students should find the following:

- A is a good solid answer.
- B is actually better than it needs to be at Stage 7, showing a developed explanation that would be suitable for Stages 8 and 9.
- C is the weakest and lacks any quotations.

Finally give out Worksheet 7.4c, which gives an annotated response to Task 4. Ask students to decide on a band for it using the grid on page 195 of the Student Book. First, ask them to consider the left-hand column of the table. This is about the sense of purpose and audience. Some of the annotations flag up whether or not the piece of writing is clearly suited to its audience and whether features of a news article are used. Students could add more if they see other features or evidence. From this they should reach a judgement about whether this suitability is clear 'sometimes', 'often' or 'always', and decide which band the answer falls in. The information on the right-hand column will remind students of the difference between a story, which is driven by events and character development, and a description, which is mainly sensory and atmospheric in purpose.

Applying the skills

Once students' responses have been reliably marked, hand out another copy of Worksheet 7.3c to each student and ask them to conduct a self-review, looking at their own strengths and weaknesses and ticking the appropriate column for their performance. From this they should be able to identify their weakest areas and note target question types for improvement.

Students could then look back at the skills icons against those questions (completed in Topic 7.2) and make a list of revisions that they want to make and sections of the book that they should revisit.

Student Book
Q3 & Q4

Use the grid below to plan your answer to Question 3. Think of things that are unusual and would make your personal story stand out. Then carry out the tasks below the table.

Diary (today's events)	Journal (current feelings)	Biography (information about other people)	Autobiography (information about yourself)

Which of your events would you find it easiest to write about? Why?

_____

_____

Which event would you find it hardest to write about? Why?

_____

_____

Which event do you think others would be most interested in reading about? Why?

_____

_____

Student Book **Q8** Look at the descriptive words below and at the two starter sentences beneath them. Write each the descriptive word below the appropriate starter sentence.

miraculous   boring   stomped   relief   desperate

humming   stubborn   sighed   endless   pointless

frustrating   patience   beautiful   industrious   obviously   charming

silent   peaceful   alarm   amazing   careful

reward   dark   cold   glow   precious   slowly

I always feel grumpy when I am getting ready for school.	I am fascinated by the art of bee-keeping.

Cambridge Checkpoint English Stage 7

Student Book
Q1–Q4

Practise your understanding of inference, deduction, explicit and implicit meaning.

Deduce what the situation is from each of these sets of information.

The sun was shining through the window. The birds were chirping in the trees. The smell of hot coffee floated up the stairs.

Situation:

_____

_____

_____

She banged as loudly as she could on the door. She knew her mother wouldn't be home for another hour. She wished she hadn't been in such a rush to leave this morning.

Situation:

_____

_____

_____

Infer what the speaker really means in each of the following examples.

'That's fine with me.' (said with a sigh)

_____

'That's fine with me.' (said in a quiet voice)

_____

'That's fine with me.' (said in a cheerful way)

_____

Change the meaning in the following statements from explicit to implicit.

For example: *She has red hair. = Her hair glows like the flames of a burning fire.*

He is a dishonest man.

_____

She was frustrated with how long it was taking.

_____

Student Book
Preparation

Recap the skills covered in Topics 1.1, 1.2 and 1.3. Draw lines to match the key term on the left with the correct definitions on the right.

diary	comparison that describes one thing as though it is another
journal	working out the writer's suggestions through their words
biography	using key words to find specific information in a text
autobiography	adding up bits of information to find an overall meaning
skimming	words that tell the reader something directly
scanning	the story of someone's life, written by someone else
point of view	individual ideas presented in a text
big idea	an opening sentence that gives clues to the message
small point	the story of someone's life, written by themselves
starter sentence	a personal opinion or way of looking at something
inference	a daily account of events and actions
deduction	an on-going account of thoughts and feelings
explicit	quickly understanding a text without reading every word
implicit	comparison between two things using 'as' or 'like'
simile	the overall meaning or message in a text
metaphor	words which gives clues that the reader must work out

Student Book **Q5**   Practise the reading skills you have learned by answering the following exam-style questions.

1   Which **two** facts about Laurie Lee's experience of moving house in the First World War are correct? Tick (✓) two answers.

- He moved house in English wintertime.

- He was scared by the experience of arriving in the new village.

- When he arrives in the village, he is left on his own.

- He is standing in a forest.

2   Write three phrases which show that Laurie finds the new place threatening.

_____

_____

_____

3   Find the simile in the last sentence.

_____

Explain what this simile means.

_____

_____

Cambridge Checkpoint English Stage 7

Student Book **Q5**

To express a particular emotion in your writing, you need to use a variety of words that are linked to that emotion. They could be synonyms for a particular word, adjectives or adverbs that describe the emotion, or images. Together these words create a semantic field.

1 Write as many synonyms for the word 'happy' as you can think of. Then use a dictionary to find a few more.

   _____

   _____

2 Choose three suitable synonyms for the word 'happy' in this sentence:

   My mum is happy that I have cleaned my bedroom.

   _____

   _____

3 Separate the words below into two semantic fields. Underline the words linked to **bored** and circle the words linked to **worried**.

slouched	sigh	frown	pacing	twiddling fingers
staring out of the window		looking up and down		biting her nails
slowly	quietly	quickly	absent-mindedly	reluctantly
grey	brisk	bland	dull	concerned	fidgeting

Student Book **Q5**   Change the following sentences from being in the present to being in the past. For example: *I walk to the beach. = I walked to the beach.*

I eat my dinner.

_____

She sits on the bench.

_____

He lifts the box.

_____

Now complete the table.

Present	Past	Past perfect	Past continuous
I write	*I wrote*	*I had written*	*I was writing*
they break			
you see			
she jumps			
we play			
he works			
I laugh			
you drive			
they clap			
she sleeps			
he speaks			
they fall			
I forget			

Cambridge Checkpoint English
Stage 7

Student Book
Q1–Q4

Practise using adjectives and adverbs with the following activities.

1   Match up adjectives and nouns from the two groups below to create descriptive pairs of words.

red   ugly   dangerous   scary   cat   rollercoaster   house   car

creaky   dry   painful   brilliant   curry   scholar   exam   joke

_____   _____

_____   _____

_____   _____

_____   _____

_____   _____

_____   _____

_____   _____

_____   _____

2   Fill in the gaps in the following sentences with the most appropriate adverb from the box.

reluctantly   briskly   unsurprisingly   miserably   mysteriously   shyly

She walked _____ down the path.

_____ the cat did not want to sleep in the same bed as the dog.

She asked him to dance rather _____.

They _____ agreed that they would tidy up before going out to play.

He disappeared as _____ as he had arrived.

She stared _____ out of the window at the falling rain.

Cambridge Checkpoint English
Stage 7

Student Book Q5 Carry out the following activities to assess the anecdote you wrote about a moment in your past.

- Annotate your paragraph to identify the different words types you have used. Use different coloured pens to underline the words and then mark the word type using the following key:

  V = verb

  N = noun

  PN = proper noun

  adv = adverb

  adj = adjective

- Use two different coloured highlighter pens to highlight simple sentences and compound sentences.

- Circle all the connectives.

- Write a conclusion about your work using the following writing frames:

Looking at my work, I have discovered _____

_____

_____

_____

_____

To improve my work, I need to _____

_____

_____

_____

_____

Student Book **Q5**   Copy the sentences below into the table to identify which assessment elements relate to which areas of learning.

- Spelling of common words is correct.
- The style of writing is correct and suitable for the audience.
- Links within and between sentences are effective.
- Paragraphs are in a good sequence, giving the overall text clear meaning.
- More difficult and adventurous vocabulary is generally spelt correctly.
- Use of punctuation is accurate.
- There is a clear viewpoint which is developed throughout the text.
- There are different types of sentences, used for effect.
- Links between paragraphs are effective.
- Punctuation is used to make meaning clear.

Purpose and audience	Text structure	Sentence structure	Punctuation	Spelling

Identifying the features of an online news report

Student Book **Q2**   Use the information in the Student Book to complete the following tasks.

- Complete the missing labels for the numbered features of the text below.
- Underline the features that information texts share.
- Put a star by the features that are specific to online news stories.

1

4

6

2

7

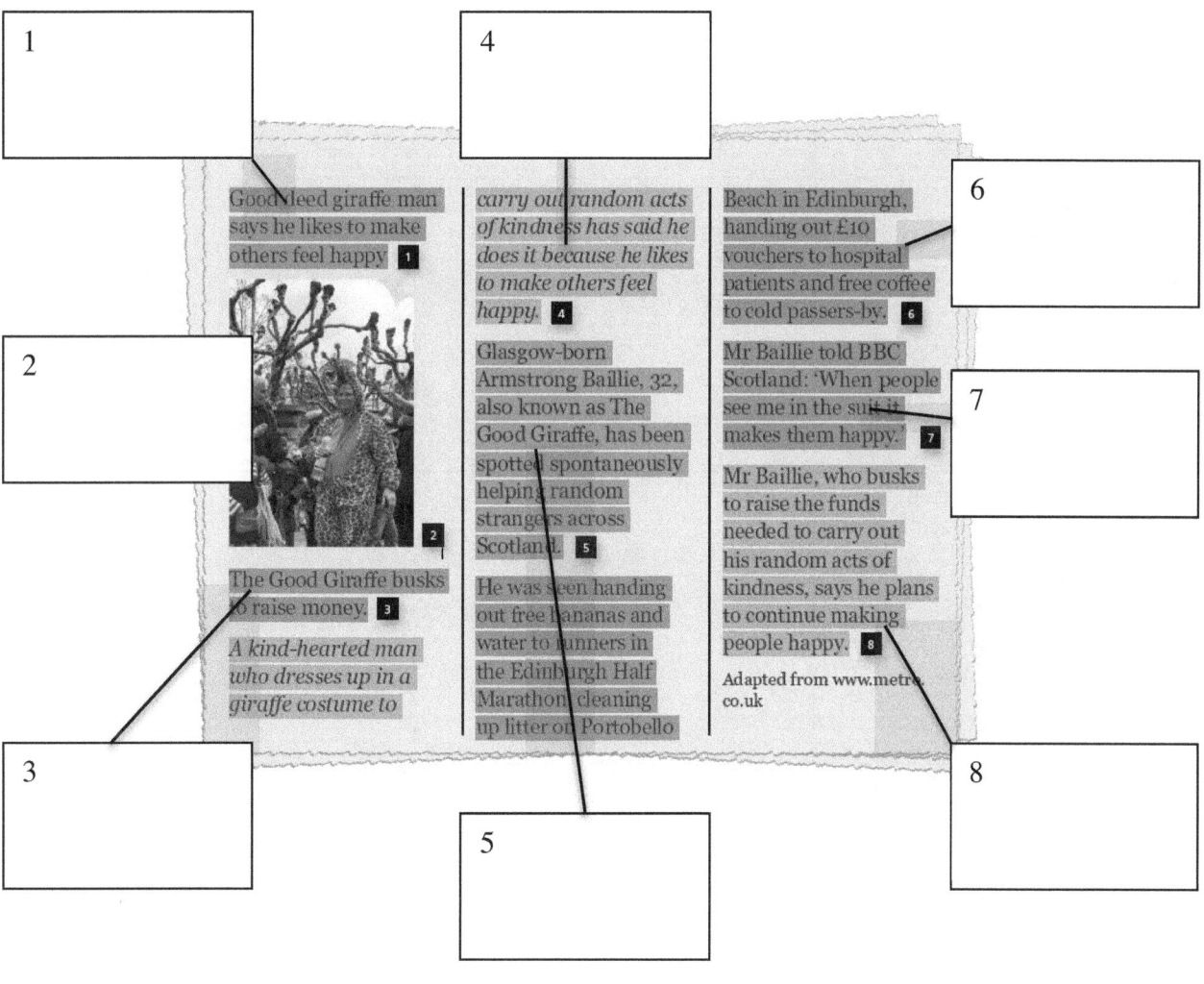

Good deed giraffe man says he likes to make others feel happy **1**

carry out random acts of kindness has said he does it because he likes to make others feel happy. **4**

Beach in Edinburgh, handing out £10 vouchers to hospital patients and free coffee to cold passers-by. **6**

Glasgow-born Armstrong Baillie, 32, also known as The Good Giraffe, has been spotted spontaneously helping random strangers across Scotland. **5**

Mr Baillie told BBC Scotland: 'When people see me in the suit it makes them happy.' **7**

2

The Good Giraffe busks to raise money. **3**

A kind-hearted man who dresses up in a giraffe costume to

He was seen handing out free bananas and water to runners in the Edinburgh Half Marathon, cleaning up litter on Portobello

Mr Baillie, who busks to raise the funds needed to carry out his random acts of kindness, says he plans to continue making people happy. **8**

Adapted from www.metro.co.uk

3

5

8

Cambridge Checkpoint English
Stage 7

Student Book **Q3** Decide which features you should search for to answer each question in the grid below. Then scan the text on page 36 of the Student Book to find the information and complete the grid.

Question	Answer	What feature(s) helped you find this information?
a) On which day of the week did the 'chain' break?		
b) How many people successfully completed the chain?		
c) Why did the Starbucks' spokesperson believe the 'chain' broke?		
d) What was the name of the Starbucks' spokesperson?		

Student Book **Q5** Read Texts A, B and C again and find examples of the features listed. Record your findings in the grid below.

Feature	Text A	Text B	Text C
abbreviations	None	*I'm*	
expressive punctuation			
slang and idioms			
official terms and names			

Student Book
Q1–3

Complete these tasks to find evidence in the text *Target Employee's Good Deed Goes Viral* that will help you decide whether the journalist is suitable for the job at *Top Stories*.

Read the story and sum it up in your own words below:

The story is about _____

_____

Complete the grid.

Question	Your answer
1 a) Who posted the story online?	
1 b) Where did the event happen?	
1 c) How many people liked the story?	
1 d) Will *Top Stories* readers find the content of this story engaging and touching? (Why?)	
2 a) Which conventions of an online news report has the journalist included?	
2 b) Name any conventions of an online news report that are missing.	
2 c) How well does the image suit the text's audience and purpose?	
3 a) Find two pieces of evidence that show whether the writer has written in formal or informal English.	1 2
3 b) How well will this article suit 'English-speaking adults all over the world'?	

Cambridge Checkpoint English
Stage 7

Student Book **Q1**   If you are the interviewer, complete grid A.

If you are the interviewee, complete grid B.

A	Work out questions for each bullet point on page 46 of the Student Book. Then decide what order you will ask your questions and number them in that order.

B	Make a note of what you will say in response to each bullet point on page 46 of the Student Book.
What the good deed was	
What happened when the good deed was carried out	
Details about the people involved – their full names, ages, and so on.	
Where events happened	
How the people involved feel about their part in the event	

Mapping your report

Student Book
Q3–Q9

Plan your online news report by filling in the grids below.

Question 3

Question	Details to include in the article
What was the good deed?	
How was the good deed done?	
Why did the person do the good deed?	
What happened as a result?	

Questions 4 and 5

Full name	Age	Home town	Country	Reaction

Questions 6–9

Connective	Main point	Details

Controlling ideas through sentence types

Student Book **Q2**   Following the instructions in the Student Book, practise forming detailed simple sentences about the people involved in your news story.

Full name (Subject)	Age	Place	Verb	Object	Time

Student Book **Q3**   Following the instructions in the Student Book, use the grid below to practise forming different types of sentences to write in your report.

First clause	Conjunction	Second clause

Cambridge Checkpoint English
Stage 7

Student Book **Q1**   Label the example of direct speech below to show the correct features from a) to d).

Precious Bonita said, 'The blaze was a nightmare. I am so grateful to Ariana for making my dream wedding possible.'

Student Book **Q2**   Add the five missing punctuation marks to the direct speech below.

Rose Oladatun, aged 80, said i hope Precious' marriage is as happy as mine was

Student Book **Q5**

Read the annotations on Response 1 in the Student Book. Then write notes and suggestions on the text below to show how you will improve it.

Read the 'Comment on Response 1' in the Student Book. Then add more notes and suggestions on the text below to show how you will improve it.

Read progress points 5b–7b in the 'Check your progress' section. Note any more changes you can make to the text below.

Use all your notes and suggestions to help you write an improved version of the article.

Teenagers are doing One Good Deed Every Day.

Teacher Brett Mark, 50, from England set up the challenge.

Teenagers have bought hamburgers for homeless people, found

owners of dropped wallets and rescued trapped animals. 'My

favourite good deed was helping parents find their toddler.'

Teenagers can record their good deeds on the OGDED

website. They have to prove they did the deed. Photographs

can be uploaded.

Cambridge Checkpoint English
Stage 7

Student Book **Q6**

Using the start of the spider diagram below, plan your opening paragraph for the home page of a zoo's website. Remember – you are trying to persuade people to come to visit the zoo.

Then fill in the gaps in the text below to complete your paragraph.

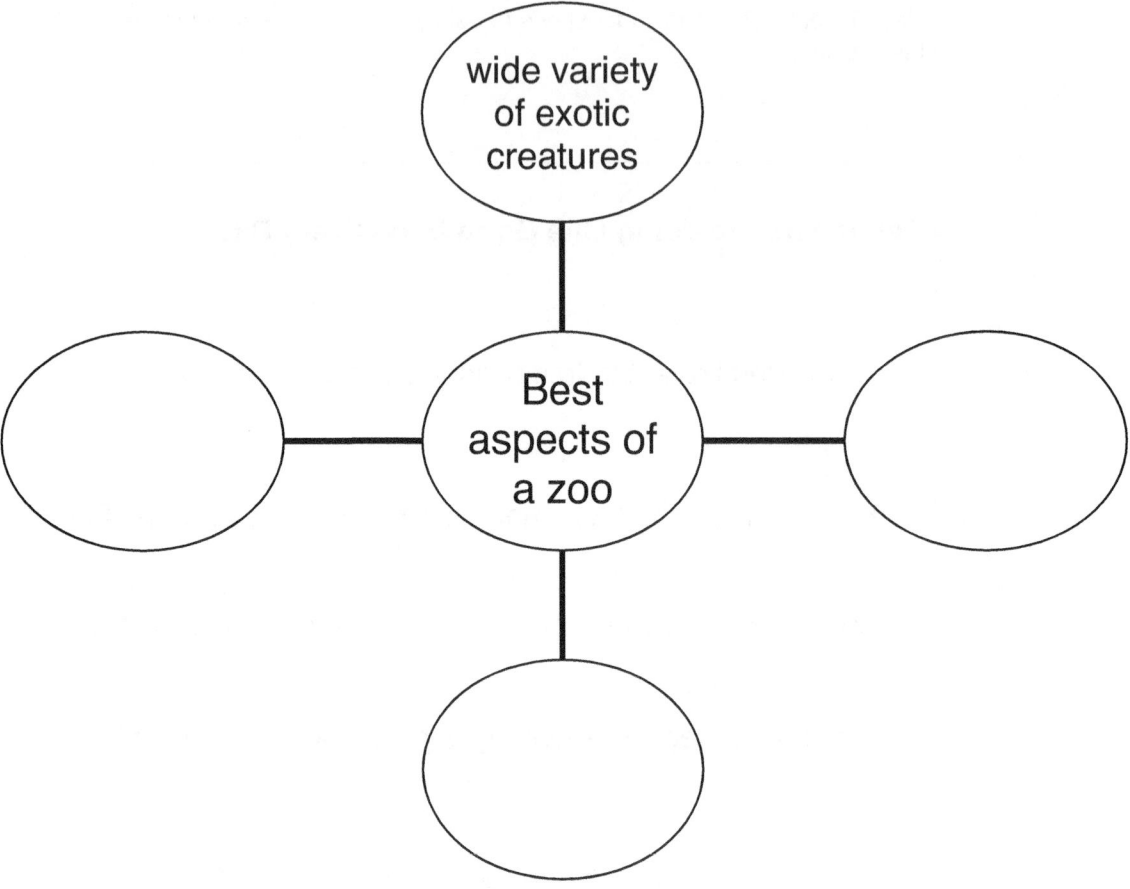

At _____ Zoo, you will be sure to find

_____.

Not only do we _____,

but we also _____.

This is the best place to _____.

If you visit us, then be certain to _____.

Identifying persuasive words

Student Book
Q11

Read the following extract and highlight any powerful words or phrases. Then choose **one** of your highlighted words/phrases and use it to complete the grid.

> Why do zoos matter? Basically, because we care. Because we want to keep this planet's amazing wildlife around for future generations.

Word/phrase choice	
This means…	
This hints at…	
Therefore, the writer implies that zoos are…	

Student Book **Q4** Arrange the words in the quotation **'even bigger spectacle'** on the continuum from strong to weak. Then decide which of the words is the 'power' word – the most emotive or powerful word in the phrase. Explain your decision below.

STRONG [ ] [ ] [ ] **WEAK**

_____

_____

_____

_____

_____

_____

Student Book **Q4** Read the extract from the passage. Then use it to write your own question asking about how the writer uses language.

Highlight the most powerful words in the passage, and then decide what these words are describing. This will be the focus of your question – the word you use to fill the blank in the question frame below.

> The Orangutan Foundation protects the orangutan but also recognises that their habitat is unique in its richness of biodiversity and crucial for local communities who are as dependent on the forest as the orangutan.

How does the writer use language to _____?

Now write an answer to the question.

_____

_____

_____

_____

_____

_____

_____

_____

_____

_____

_____

Student Book
Q10

Use the grids below to help you contribute to the discussion.

FOR zoos	
Argument	**Evidence**
Zoos educate the public.	At the Saint Louis Zoo, about 400,000 children and adults participate in our formal programs, including classes and Camp KangaZoo each year.
Zoos save endangered species.	Only 23 Amur leopards are left in the wild because of poaching and habitat destruction and they're only being kept alive because of breeding programmes in zoos.
Zoos have breeding programmes.	
Visiting a zoo is a family activity.	London Zoo runs the 'Little Creatures Family Festival' in August every year.

AGAINST zoos	
Argument	**Evidence**
Animals suffer ill health and become unfit.	A study of UK zoos, found that 75% of elephants were overweight and only 16% could walk normally, the remainder having various degrees of lameness.
Animals suffer stress and boredom.	Tigers and lions have around 18,000 times less space in zoos than they would in the wild.
Some zoos kill their surplus animals.	Copenhagen Zoo killed a young giraffe to prevent 'in breeding'.

Student Book
Extension

An adverbial clause is a group of words that plays the role of an adverb. It can be used to link the main idea and the supporting idea in a complex sentence. For example:

- *Ultimately*, we care about animal welfare. (normal adverb)
- *At the end of the day*, we care about animal welfare. (adverbial clause)

Rewrite the following sentences, changing the adverb to an adverbial clause.

The animals' needs are looked after carefully.

_____

_____

Basically, zoos need to be shut down.

_____

_____

Fortunately, modern zoos provide space and freedom for their animals.

_____

_____

Cambridge Checkpoint English
Stage 7

Student Book **Q9**   Identify and label persuasive devices in the text below. See if you can find examples of:

- personal pronouns
- the rule of three
- emotive language.

> Tigers, elephants and orang-utans are beautiful creatures and should be saved from extinction. These animals are dying out because of humans and this is unfair.
>
> Firstly, humans have been destroying the habitats of creatures around the world. For example, orang-utans have been displaced from the forests of Indonesia and Malaysia due to human production of palm oil, illegal open cast mining and illegal logging. Humans are killing orang-utans just so that they can make more money.
>
> Another reason innocent creatures are becoming extinct is due to humans taking animals out of the wild for the exotic pet trade. According to WWF, there are more tigers living in American gardens than in the wild. It is estimated that at least 5,000 tigers are kept captive in the USA, but there are as few as 3,200 tigers left in their natural habitats. This is a shocking statistic that reveals that humans are more concerned with using animals as status symbols, than with protecting them. In addition to this, many of the people who privately own tigers in the USA are not trained to look after animals. Consequently these powerful creatures could be neglected, abused and mishandled.
>
> Some people might argue that species dying out is part of the evolutionary cycle and that is natural for some less successful creatures to become extinct as the world changes around them.
>
> However, this is not the case for the majority of these creatures. There is no evolutionary reason for elephants to become extinct. They are only at risk because of poaching, conflict with humans and habitat loss.
>
> In conclusion, our world's biodiversity is under threat and we need to do something about it. If we do not take action, then elephants, orang-utans, tigers and many more beautiful creatures will die out. We must act now, or we will lose these endangered species forever.

Now write your own sentences about zoos, using these persuasive devices.

_____

_____

_____

_____

_____

Student Book **Q2** Write a letter to a newspaper, which argues either for or against keeping animals in zoos. Start by completing the planning grid below.

Paragraph	Focus on…	Evidence
1		
2		
3		
4		
5		
6		

Explaining the effects of descriptive language

Student Book **Q7** Using the writing frames below, explain the three different descriptive techniques and how the words or techniques have an effect on the reader.

In the extract about the cave, a _____

is used to describe _____. This gets

across the idea that _____.

The extract also uses _____ to describe

_____. This is effective because it

makes the reader imagine _____.

Lastly, _____ is described by

using _____. This is a good description because

it helps the reader _____

_____.

Student Book **Q3**   Cut out the cards below and match up the statements, quotations and comments.

The twins are impressed by their first sight of the sphere.	'sparkling staircase'	The simile compares the children to tiny insects, suggesting what they look like in comparison to the sphere.
The sphere looked very big.	'The twins gasped.'	This adjective suggests that it is so clean that it reflects the light.
The staircase is very clean.	'the two of them climbing up like tiny ants'	The adjective 'enormous' and the comparison to a large building shows how big the sphere is.
The children feel small next to the sphere.	'an enormous glass sphere, the size of St Paul's Cathedral'	The verb 'gasped' suggests that the sight of the sphere took their breath away.

Cambridge Checkpoint English
Stage 7

Explaining how writers use different techniques in description

Student Book Q3   Using the example annotations for the underlined words and phrases to help you, annotate the bold text to explore the different techniques that the writer has used to create a harsh, wintry setting and develop an atmosphere of fear.

Ser Waymar looked him over with open disapproval. 'I am not going back to Castle Black a failure on my first ranging. We will find these men.' He glanced around. 'Up the tree. **Be quick about it.** Look for a fire.'

Will turned away, wordless. There was no use to argue. The wind was moving. It cut right through him. He went to the tree, a vaulting grey-green sentinel, and began to climb. Soon his hands were sticky with sap, and he was lost among the needles. **Fear filled his gut like a meal he could not digest...**

> **Metaphor:** the comparison makes the wind seem dangerous.

Down below, the lordling called out suddenly, 'Who goes there?' Will heard uncertainty in the challenge. He stopped climbing; **he listened; he watched**.

> **Adverb:** 'suddenly' makes the reader feel how on edge the characters must be.

The woods gave answer: the rustle of leaves, the **icy** rush of the stream, a distant hoot of a snow owl.

The Others made no sound.

> **Onomatopoeia:** the sound helps the reader imagine the setting. It is eerily quiet and the sudden noise of the bird might scare Will.

Will saw movement from the corner of his eye. **Pale shapes gliding** through the wood. He turned his head, glimpsed a **white shadow** in the darkness. **Then it was gone.** Branches stirred gently in the wind, **scratching at one another with wooden fingers**. Will opened his mouth to call down a warning, and the words seemed to **freeze** in his throat. Perhaps he was wrong. Perhaps it had only been a bird, a reflection on the **snow**, some trick of the moonlight. What had he seen, after all?

> **Rhetorical question:** Will is questioning his surroundings; he is anxious and feels in danger.

'Will, where are you?' Ser Waymar called up. 'Can you see anything?' He was turning in a slow circle, suddenly wary, his sword in hand. He must have felt them, as Will felt them. **There was nothing to see.** 'Answer me! **Why is it so cold?'**

It was cold. Shivering, Will clung more tightly to his perch. His face pressed hard against the trunk of the sentinel. He could feel the sweet, sticky sap on his cheek.

A shadow emerged from the dark of the wood.

From *A Game of Thrones* by George R.R. Martin

Student Book
Starter

Read the short paragraph below. Annotate the text by identifying the different features that the writer uses to create a creepy atmosphere. Then add to your ideas by commenting on the *effect* of the features you have identified – *how* do they make the atmosphere creepy?

> The child stood in the vast, shadowy corridor, feeling the darkness pressing against him. His heart beat fast like a panicked drum as he looked around. Terror stopped his breath. From somewhere in the blackness, he heard a man laughing.

_____

_____

_____

_____

_____

_____

_____

_____

_____

Cambridge Checkpoint English
Stage 7

Student Book **Q5** Using a thesaurus, find five alternatives for each of the words listed below. Think about how each of your chosen words gives additional meaning to the original word.

good

-
-
-
-
-

bad

-
-
-
-
-

move

-
-
-
-
-

eat

-
-
-
-
-

look

-
-
-
-
-

think

-
-
-
-
-

Student Book
Q11

Use the writing frame to help you include a range of sentence structures when describing your entry into the skyscraper.

Opening the huge doors nervously, we _____

_____

< Complete this complex sentence, describing going into the skyscraper.

We saw _____ and we could hear

_____

< Now complete this compound sentence to describe what you saw and heard in the skyscraper.

Climbing the first staircase, we _____

_____ .

< Next, complete this complex sentence to describe what you did.

There was _____

< Add a simple sentence to create a shock.

Even though we were terrified, we _____

_____ .

< Follow this with a complex sentence to say what you did in response.

_____

_____

< End your description with a complex sentence and a compound sentence of your own.

_____

Student Book **Q7** Plan four paragraphs of a piece of writing that describes your own arrival in the futuristic city.

Your first paragraph should be a general description of the scene.

Add ideas for the next three paragraphs. Use this table to help with your planning.

Paragraph	Focus on...
1) the general scene (a description of the city as a whole)	
2)	
3)	
4)	

Student Book **Q1 & Q2**

Complete a spider diagram of your futuristic landscape or city.

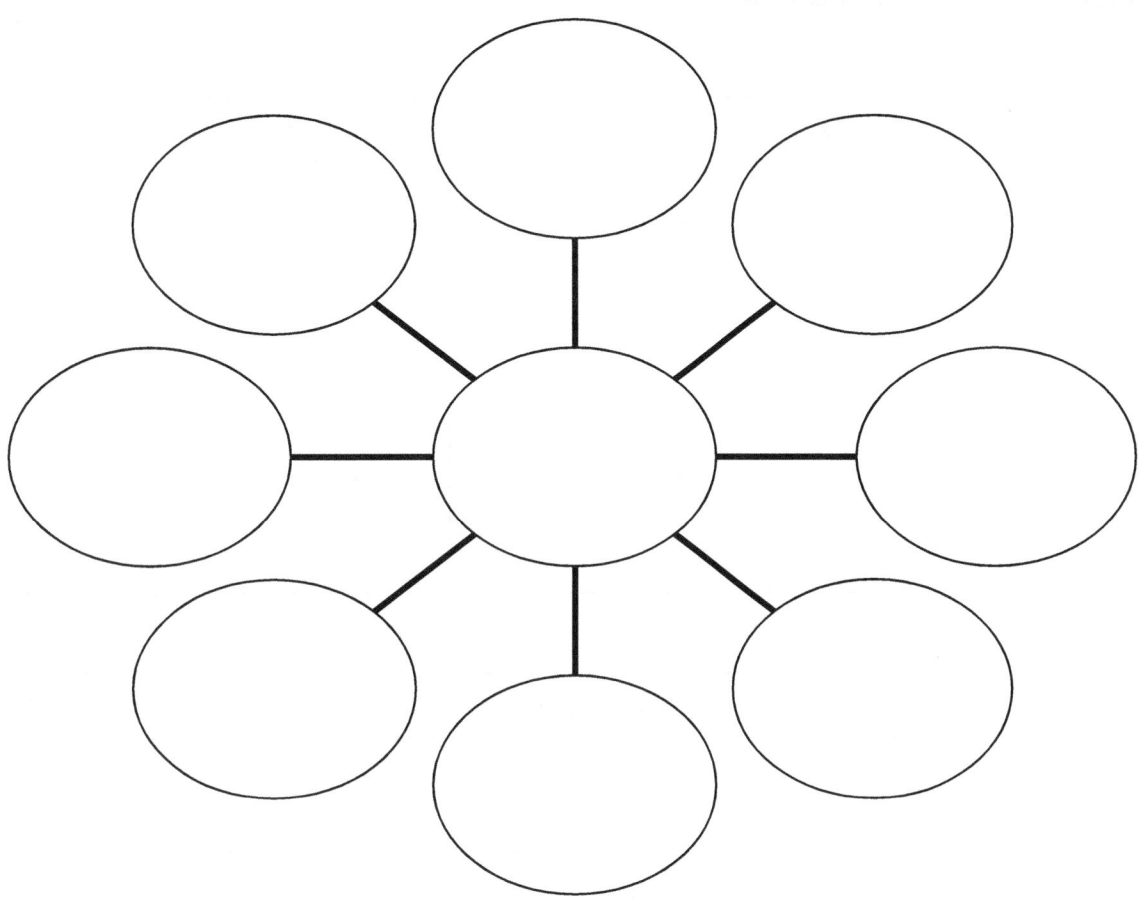

Use the table to plan and sequence your paragraphs.

Paragraph	Focus on...
1)	
2)	
3)	
4)	

Cambridge Checkpoint English Stage 7

Student Book Starter & Q1

Use the information in the Student Book to identify the features of narrative and non-narrative texts.

Narrative	Non-narrative

Text	Narrative or non-narrative text?
dictionary	
novel	
encyclopedia	
newspaper article	
short story	
autobiography	
recipe book	

Student Book **Q1**   Circle the words that could describe the house in the picture.

<table>
<tr><td>old</td><td>charming</td><td>decrepit</td><td>delightful</td></tr>
<tr><td>sinister</td><td>creepy</td><td>fantastic</td><td>dilapidated</td></tr>
<tr><td>overgrown</td><td>decayed</td><td>idyllic</td><td>ugly</td></tr>
</table>

Explain why you have chosen three of these adjectives.

Adjective	Explanation

Now think of three more adjectives to describe the house and write them below.

1 _____

2 _____

3 _____

Student Book **Q4** Look at the lists of adjectives below. Draw lines to link each word to its opposite.

strong	careless
cheerful	rough
brave	clumsy
careful	cowardly
nimble	weak
fair	serious
kind	miserable
gentle	unequal
carefree	unpleasant

Now order the words into two columns: one to describe an overall positive character, and the other an overall negative character:

Positive	Negative

Student Book **Q1** Read this passage. Some of the words have been left out. Add your own choice of words to create a cold and miserable setting.

Once upon a time – of all the good days in the year, on Christmas Eve – old

Scrooge sat busy in his counting-house. It was cold, _____,

biting weather: foggy withal: and he could hear the people in the court outside, go

_____ up and down, beating their hands upon their

breasts, and stamping their feet upon the pavement stones to warm them. The

city clocks had only just gone three, but it was quite _____

already – it had not been light all day – and candles were flaring in the windows

of the neighbouring offices, like _____ smears upon the

_____ brown air. The fog came pouring in at every chink

and keyhole, and was so dense without, that although the court was of the

narrowest, the houses opposite were mere phantoms. To see the

_____ cloud come drooping down, obscuring

everything, one might have thought that Nature lived hard by, and was brewing

on a large scale.

Student Book **Q1**   In each section of the flow diagram, list the type of information you would expect to see in each part of a story arc.

Beginning

- _____
- _____
- _____
- _____

Middle

- _____
- _____
- _____
- _____

End

- _____
- _____
- _____
- _____

Student Book **Q5** Read the extract. Underline the words and phrases that show that this is a mysterious setting. Aim to underline at least three words or phrases.

There was no one in the room. But under the window stood a low, white, marble table, and draped from one end, as though it had been jerked off, was a tapestry of cloth of gold. Roland went to the table. It was quite plain, except for the shape of a sword cut deep in the stone. He picked up the golden tapestry and spread it over the table. It dropped with the folds of long, untouched use, and the impression of the sword was in the cloth.

Add annotations to explain why you find these words and phrases effective.

Try to use the key words you have learned: 'narrative', 'viewpoint', 'structure' and 'suspense'.

Cambridge Checkpoint English Stage 7

Student Book
Q2 & Q3

Complete the grids to record Cecily's and Miss Peabody's feelings at different points in the narrative. Remember that they are very different characters with different thoughts and feelings.

First, circle the adjectives that best describe Cecily. Then in a different colour, circle the adjectives that best describe Miss Peabody.

kind   cruel   thoughtful

selfish   sensible   vulnerable

Now write down Cecily's thoughts and feelings before, during and after seeing her brother.

Before	
During	
After	

Now write down Miss Peabody's thoughts and feelings at the same points in the narrative.

Before	
During	
After	

Student Book **Q3**   Use the grid below to make notes on your story by answering the questions. Then add your ideas to your spider diagram.

Plot	What happens in the story?	
	What is the end goal of your story?	
	What obstacles must be overcome to reach it?	
Character	Who is involved in the story?	
	What are they like?	
	What are their relationships with one another?	
Setting	Where does the story take place?	
	What does this place look like?	
	Where is it in space and time?	

Cambridge Checkpoint English
Stage 7

Student Book
Q1 & Q2

Different punctuation marks create different effects in speech.

Which punctuation mark indicates surprise? Circle your choice.

?   !   ()   \

Which punctuation mark indicates confusion? Circle your choice.

?   !   ()   \

Add punctuation to this extract to show which characters are speaking and how they are speaking.

A merry Christmas, uncle God save you cried a cheerful voice. It was the voice of Scrooge's nephew, who came upon him so quickly that this was the first intimation he had of his approach.

Bah said Scrooge Humbug

He had so heated himself with rapid walking in the fog and frost, this nephew of Scrooge's, that he was all in a glow; his face was ruddy and handsome; his eyes sparkled, and his breath smoked again. Christmas a humbug, uncle said Scrooge's nephew. You don't mean that, I am sure

I do said Scrooge. Merry Christmas What right have you to be merry What reason have you to be merry You're poor enough

Come, then returned the nephew gaily. What right have you to be dismal What reason have you to be morose You're rich enough

Student Book
Starter

Sort the connectives below into the correct columns of the grid.

then	now	when	however	but

which	for	afterwards	soon

next	later	finally	sometimes

Time connectives	Order and argument connectives

Student Book
Q4 & Q5

Add notes to the spider diagram to plan your story.

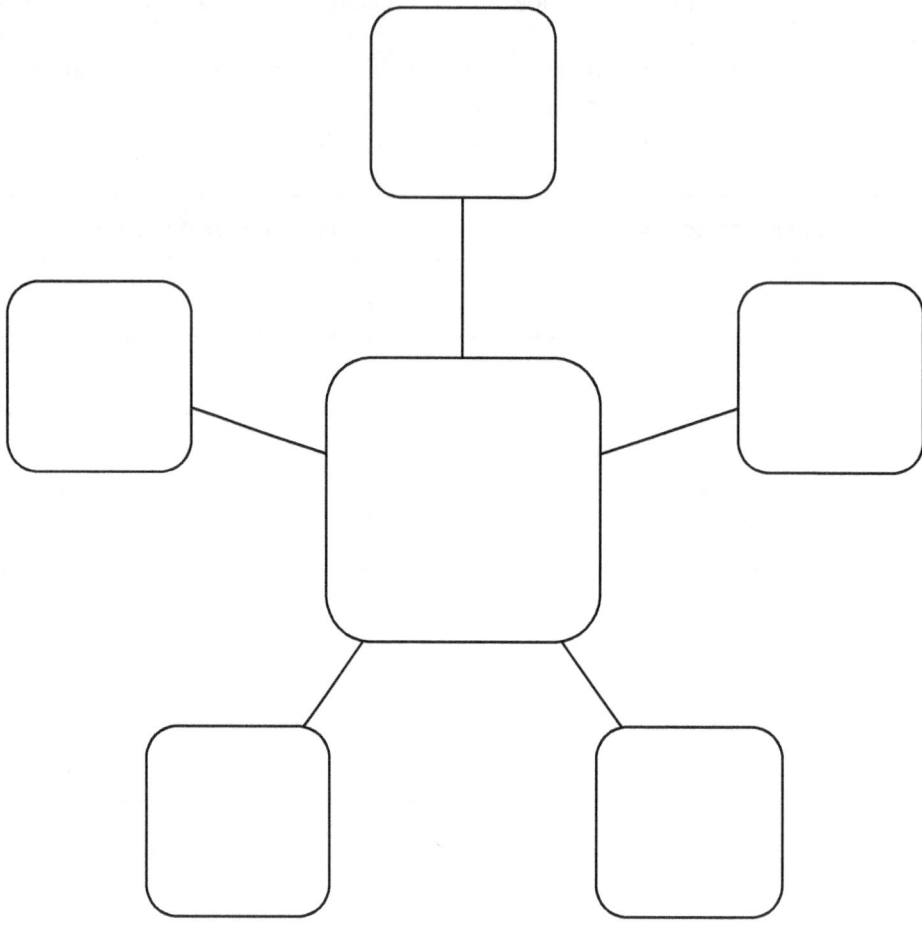

Label the notes on your diagram with whether they relate to plot, setting or character.

Planning paragraphs in reviews

Student Book Q4 Re-read Lia's review of 'Beauty and the Beast' in the Student Book, then complete the grid. Decide on the focus of each paragraph (the main thing it was about) and what Lia seemed to think. Finally, add any evidence (actual lines from the review) that support this.

Paragraph	Focus (if any)	Comment/analysis	Evidence
1			
2	The acting of Paolo and Rita.	Lia thought it was good that the audience could hear their words. She thought Paolo was very believable as a monster.	'spoke clearly and with real emotion' 'really frightened us'
3	The set design, in particular the staircase.		
4	The costumes, in particular those of…		
5	None – she is summing up what she feels.		

Cambridge Checkpoint English
Stage 7

Student Book **Q8**

Read the story extract below, then mark the following changes to help you turn it into a play script:

- **Verbs** that you may need to change from **past** to **present** tense forms

- **Speech marks** that need removing from spoken lines

- **Characters' thoughts** or any other information that cannot be included in a play script

- **Names** that need to be moved

- **Anything else** you notice

> Delete speech marks

> Change to 'weeps' or 'weeping'.

> Change to 'enters' or 'entering'.

Beauty was desperate for news of her family, and <u>wept and wept</u>. Quietly, the Beast <u>entered</u> her room.

<u>'What is it?'</u> he asked, tenderly, his growl less severe than before.

'I…miss my family,' she said, sadly.

Beast held out a mirror. It sparkled in the light and seemed to change colour as Beauty took it from his rough hands.

'Here,' he said. 'Look into the mirror and it will tell you all you need to know.'

Slowly, he paced out of the room.

Student Book **Q6**   Use the grid below to check how well people in the group are using their discussion skills. Tick the boxes for each student taking part when they show a particular skill.

Name of each student in the group	Took turns	Didn't interrupt; wasn't rude	Encouraged others	Spoke politely	Stuck to the point	Gave reasons for point of view

Assessing your own discussion skills

Student Book **Q7** Use the grid below to check your own performance in the group discussion task. Tick the boxes to give yourself a mark between 1 (low) and 5 (high) for each category.

In the group task, how well did you...	1	2	3	4	5
take turns?					
avoid interrupting?					
encourage others?					
speak politely?					
stick to the point?					
give reasons for your point of view?					

Student Book **Q4**   Read the poem, then draw lines to match any gothic features to particular parts of the poem.

In a Far Land

In a far land
a black mountain broods:
beneath the black mountain
stretch the green woods.

Among the green woods
a white castle soars:
in the white castle
are dark corridors.

The corridors lead
to a black, shut door.
Behind it a Prince
sprawls dead on the floor.

With a cobwebbed cup
by his withered hand,
a Prince lies poisoned
in that far land.

A hobbling old Princess
creeps to that door –
ghost calling ghost
for evermore!

She murmurs her guilt
In sighs and soft moans.
Behind the locked door
the dead Prince groans.

by Raymond Wilson

forest and/or mountain setting

mysterious plot (murder, revenge, etc.)

good characters turned bad

supernatural happenings

Cambridge Checkpoint English
Stage 7

Student Book **Q8**   Cut out the cards, mix them up and ask students to select appropriate connectives to place at the start of the second sentence. Write or display the whole paragraph on a screen or large sheet of paper so students can try out different choices.

In the same way	Similarly	As well as	Both
In contrast	However	Yet	In the last verse
Initially	Next	Later	Firstly
To start with	Then	After that	But
Finally	At the end	At the conclusion	Afterwards

Student Book **Q1**   Use these copies of the poems to make notes.

The Magic Seeds

There was an old woman who sowed a corn seed,
And from it there sprouted a tall yellow weed.
She planted the seeds of the tall yellow flower,
And up sprang a blue one in less than an hour.
The seed of the blue one she sowed in a bed,
And up sprang a tall tree with blossoms of red.
And high in the treetop there sang a white bird,
And his song was the sweetest that ever was heard.
The people they came from far and from near,
The song of the little white bird for to hear.

by James Reeves

Jack and the Beanstalk, Part 2

But overnight the tiny seeds grew and grew and grew and grew into a

H U G E

	B	the top
reached	E	
	A	till he
up	N	
	S	quickly
	T	
climbed	A	
	L	Jack
	K	which

by Mike Gould

Cambridge Checkpoint English
Stage 7

Top tips

Always read the question carefully.

Check how many marks are available for the question, as this will indicate how long your answer should be, or how many parts you should provide in your answer.

Reading questions

- Look out for questions that ask you to 'find', 'copy' or 'give a quotation'. This means you must *only* use the words written and no others.
- Remember that even if you are unsure exactly what a word means, you can often work it out from the rest of the sentence. Then do a quick check to make sure your idea fits with the rest of the text.
- If a question asks you to use your own words, then you must *not* copy or quote.
- Look out for questions that tell you how many words to find. Only find *exactly* that number.
- If you are asked to tick *one* box then you must only tick *one*. If you make an error then cross it out and tick your new choice clearly.
- If a question asks you why a writer does something, your answer should be about the *effect* that the writer wanted to have on the reader.
- If a question asks what a word *suggests*, it is asking you to draw an *inference* from the word or phrase. This means you may need to work out an emotion, attitude or atmosphere from the words used.
- Questions that ask you to *explain* are asking you to give *reasons* and *evidence*. This could be in the form of quotations, close reference or inferences that you have drawn from the text.
- Remember that a summary should be mainly in your own words and should not contain comments, examples or opinions.

Writing questions

- Remember to plan your answers. This is very important, as the ideas that you have and the way they are organised will be rewarded.
- Check your work carefully when you have finished writing. Your work is assessed for six separate things:
    - content
    - addressing the audience appropriately
    - text structure
    - sentence structure
    - punctuation
    - vocabulary and spelling.

Do not be afraid to make corrections or even add words or phrases when you are checking your writing.

	Read closely and annotate key words.
	Only use words from text.
THE SAT ON THE MAT	Use the whole sentence to work out a word's meaning.
	Only use your own words.
	Be careful to only give the number of answers asked for.
?	'Why?' means 'for what effect?'
	Find an inference.
	'Explain' means 'give reasons and evidence'.
	A summary does not have examples or detail.
	Plan!
	Check your work.

Cambridge Checkpoint English
Stage 7

Task 1

1 Which word in paragraph 1 suggests that people who think that sea cows are mermaids are wrong? (1)

2 Explain in your own words the meaning of the word 'unlikely' as it is used in paragraph 2. (1)

3 Which of these statements is a fact about sea cows? (1)

    a) Sea cows are slender and graceful.
    b) Sea cows weigh more than humans.
    c) Sea cows have arms.
    d) Sea cows have grey scales.

4 Which word in paragraph 2 suggests that sea cows are big? (1)

5 What does using the word 'But' at the start of paragraph 3 suggest? (1)

6 Which word in paragraph 3 has a suffix? (1)

7 Write a suitable sub-heading for paragraph 3. (2)

8 Find an adjective in paragraph 4 which shows that the writer did not expect manatees and mermaids to be alike. (1)

9 Write three ways in which sea cows are like humans. (2)

10 Explain in your own words the meaning of each of the following, as it is used in the text. (2)

    a) dwelling (line 13)

    b) spotted (line 22)

11 What is the main purpose of this text? (1)

12 Write down the statement that most accurately reflects what cryptozoologists think mermaids are. (1)

    a) Mermaids aren't seals or sea cows.
    b) Mermaids aren't real.
    c) Mermaids are a new type of animal.

13 Write down a phrase from paragraph 2 which shows that the writer is giving examples to make her meaning clearer. (1)

14 What is the underlined word an example of? (1)

Its discovery makes <u>us</u> wonder.

15 Write a summary of 70–90 words explaining why cryptozoology could provide the answer to the mystery of what a mermaid is. (5)

16 Why does the writer use a pair of dashes in paragraph 3? (1)

17 Divide the following complex sentence into a series of shorter ones, using any punctuation that you consider appropriate. You may change wording slightly to retain agreement and clarity. (2)

Although scientists agree that thousands of unknown animals exist – particularly insects – they criticise cryptozoologists for focusing their efforts mostly on exciting and elusive (hard to find) creatures, like mermaids, despite little scientific support for their existence.

Task 2

Write a news article for a local paper about the sighting of a possible mermaid or other creature of legend such as a unicorn or dragon.

You will need to:

- choose a creature or invent a new one
- use the language and structure of a news article to help make the information clear – for example, headline, standfirst…

Do not include illustrations or any other layout features.

Write your plan out first.

Cambridge Checkpoint English
Stage 7

Testing your skills: Planning your writing

Who is the audience for your writing task?

_____

What do you know about the type of language that is usually used for this audience?

_____

_____

What is the purpose of your writing task?

_____

_____

What do you know about the kind of language techniques which often get used to fulfil this purpose?

_____

_____

What form should your task be written in?

_____

_____

What do you know about the type of information that normally goes into this form of writing?

_____

_____

_____

What do you know about the way in which this form should be structured?

_____

_____

_____

Cambridge Checkpoint English
Stage 7

Task 3

1 Which of the statements below best sums up this extract? (1)

   a) It is about a girl who is scared of what she sees in the water.
   b) It is about a girl who begins to see what has been around her in the water all the time.
   c) It is about a girl who learns to live under water.

2 Whose viewpoint is this story told from? (1)

3 Re-read the paragraph that begins 'The sea around us began...'. In your own words, describe the way the writer has used sentence lengths and structures to describe the seals. (5)

4 The writer uses a dash once in line 17 when Sapphire is speaking to Faro. Why does the writer use this dash? (1)

5 Which word used in paragraph 11 suggests that the fish are brightly coloured? (1)

6 Read this sentence from the passage:

   I look to my left and there's a huge flatfish, as big as our kitchen table, with one popeye goggling at me.

   What two things are compared in this sentence? (1)

7 Find two examples of imagery used to describe the jellyfish. (2)

8 What do the words 'I scull backwards' suggest about Sapphire's feelings towards the jellyfish? (2)

9 Why does the writer use an ellipsis at the end of the paragraph describing the jellyfish? (1)

10 Which word in line 42 tells you that the spider crabs move quickly? (1)

11 Re-read lines 1–20. Describe the relationship between Faro and Sapphire as shown in this extract. (4)

12 How is Sapphire feeling during this extract? (5)

Task 4

In the passage you have read, Sapphire discovers a whole new world where she does not expect it.

Write a description of your own about a place where things change or are revealed that you did not expect.

You will need to consider:

- setting: where are you going to be for your description?
- character: are there any other characters?
- plot: why do things happen in this way? What do you do/feel?

Look at the following sample answers to Question 15. Decide which is the most effective and why.

A

Cryptozoology could provide the answer to the mystery of what a mermaid is because we have found other things which nobody believed were alive such as a Megamouth shark which was totally unheard of until it was found in 1976. If this is possible then it could also be possible that there are mermaids.

B

Cryptozoology could provide the answer to the mermaid mystery because it is based on the idea that anything is possible because anything might be discovered in the future. If there have been sightings, then that is because there is something out there that we just haven't caught yet! It uses past and recent discoveries of creatures, which happen all the time, once thought to be mythical or totally unknown and thought of, to suggest that we may one day find a real mermaid. Even scientists can't deny that we are always finding new creatures.

C

The first reason why cryptozoology could provide the answer is that there have been sightings of them which cannot be answered by any other theories. Secondly scientists agree that there are many undiscovered species in the world so it is possible that mermaids are one. Thirdly there is a proven history of creatures which mankind thought of as mythical, turning out to be real.

Task 2 asked you to write a news article for a local paper. Think first about what you would expect a news article to be like. How should it be structured? What sort of language would it contain?

Look at the sample response. Which band would you put this answer into? Use the annotations to help you decide.

Traffic halts as dragon swoops over local High Street [1]

Traffic came to a standstill in Selsey High Street [2] yesterday, 28 July, [3] after a large creature, said by some to be a dragon, was spotted swooping across the horizon ahead. [4]

Police and emergency services were first alerted at 3 p.m., when anxious parents collecting their children from school saw the brightly coloured giant bird hovering above The Academy playing fields. By the time the fire brigade arrived and blocked off the High Street leading to Selsey Hill, the creature was nowhere to be seen. [5]

Local resident Aneka Sanderson spoke to our reporter on the scene. She told us, 'It was huge and had a wing span of about 5 metres. They were purple and green and seemed to glow. I couldn't see its head but it looked as if it was scaly and rough.' [6]

Parents are being warned to keep children and small pets indoors until further investigations have been completed. [7]

---

[1] headline

[2] detail about where

[3] detail about when

[4] detail about what

[5] summary of the story in brief

[6] eye-witness account

[7] final summary statement

Testing your skills: Self-review

Look at the list of question types below and begin to rate yourself according to how well you did and how confident you are in your ability.

	Not great	Okay	Good	Great
questions that test location of facts and simple ideas				
questions that test understanding of simple ideas and information				
questions which use inference				
questions about the way writers use language				
questions that require summary skills				
questions where you write in a specific form				
questions where you write for a specific audience				
questions where the structuring of ideas is important				
questions where the accuracy of language is important				

Cambridge Checkpoint English
Stage 7

Look at these two responses to Question 3. Which of these answers is better? Why?

> **A**
> *There are lots of short sentences when the seals are described. Lots of the sentences start with the word 'they'.*

> **B**
> *Most of the sentences are quite similar. They all start the same and have the same simple structure. It makes it sound like she is watching them and only them and finds them amazing. The sentences that describe the seals moving are shorter than the ones about what they look like.*

_____

_____

_____

_____

_____

Look at these two responses to Question 8. Which of these answers is better? Why?

> **A**
> *Sapphire is scared and the quote shows that she moves backwards to get away.*

> **B**
> *She wants to get away.*

_____

_____

_____

_____

_____

Testing your skills: Assessing answers to Task 3 (2)

Rank these answers to Question 12 and explain the reasoning behind your decisions.

A
I think that she is feeling nervous because it says that she moved backwards and also a bit unsure because it says 'um…' I think she gets a bit annoyed when he says she didn't notice anything because she says, 'I noticed that shark...'

B
At first Sapphire is a bit uncertain of what she is seeing. She says, 'Um, is that a current…?' You say 'um' when you're trying to think and this tells us she doesn't know what it is straight away which makes us feel sorry for her. She gets quite annoyed with him when she goes on. She says, 'I noticed that shark, anyway, and you didn't.' The word 'anyway' suggests that she is defending herself a bit and putting him down.

C
The girl feels lots of different things. She is worried, irritated, then amazed by what she discovers.

_____

_____

_____

_____

_____

_____

_____

_____

_____

_____

_____

Task 4 asked you to write a description. Think first about what you would expect a piece of descriptive writing to be like. How would you expect it to be structured? What sort of language would it contain?

Look at the sample response. Which band would you put this answer into? Use the annotations to help you decide.

A place where things change

The television was off and I could hear **[1]** the distant growl of a lawn-mower in next door's garden. Looking around the lounge everything was as it usually is; the blue flowery sofa **[2]** with a brown stain **[3]** on the arm where I'd spilled my hot chocolate last week, wrestling with the dog, was still pushed up against the wall. The sea blue **[4]** cushions still all squashed **[5]** in the middle from too many pillow fights with my sister were lying randomly **[6]** as always. Only the thick velvety curtains seemed odd to me; closed on this sunny day **[7]** with ripples bulging along them as if a window was open behind them. **[8]**

My eyes dropped to the floor. The rug lay like seaweed on the beach, **[9]** stringy bits of wool stretching out from its edges as if asking to escape **[10]** from the constant chewing it got from our new puppy.

'Surprise!' I jumped as the curtain flapped towards me and my sister and Mum leapt out shouting loudly. 'Happy Birthday!' they sang as the dogs came bounding **[11]** out barking **[12]** and bouncing after their time in hiding.

---

[1] appeals to our sense of sound

[2] appeals to our sense of sight

[3] appeals to our sense of sight

[4] appeals to our sense of sight

[5] appeals to our sense of sight

[6] appeals to our sense of sight

[7] suggests texture and appeals to our sense of touch

[8] suggests movement and appeals to our sense of sight

[9] uses a simile to help us picture the rug

[10] uses personification to engage the reader

[11] suggests movement

[12] appeals to our sense of sound

Check your progress	1a	
	2a	
	3a	
	4a	
	5a	
	6a	
	7a	
	1b	
	2b	
	3b	
	4b	
	5b	
	6b	
	7b	
	1c	
	2c	
	3c	
	4c	
	5c	
	6c	
	7c	

Cambridge Checkpoint English
Stage 7

Check your progress	1a	
	2a	
	3a	
	4a	
	5a	
	6a	
	7a	
	1b	
	2b	
	3b	
	4b	
	5b	
	6b	
	7b	
	1c	
	2c	
	3c	
	4c	
	5c	
	6c	
	7c	

Check your progress	1a	
	2a	
	3a	
	4a	
	5a	
	6a	
	7a	
	1b	
	2b	
	3b	
	4b	
	5b	
	6b	
	7b	
	1c	
	2c	
	3c	
	4c	
	5c	
	6c	
	7c	

Cambridge Checkpoint English
Stage 7

Check your progress	1a	
	2a	
	3a	
	4a	
	5a	
	6a	
	1b	
	2b	
	3b	
	4b	
	5b	
	6b	
	1c	
	2c	
	3c	
	4c	
	5c	
	6c	

Check your progress		
	1a	
	2a	
	3a	
	4a	
	5a	
	6a	
	7a	
	8a	
	9a	
	1b	
	2b	
	3b	
	4b	
	5b	
	6b	
	7b	
	8b	
	9b	
	1c	
	2c	
	3c	
	4c	
	5c	
	6c	
	7c	
	8c	
	9c	

Cambridge Checkpoint English
Stage 7

Check your progress

1a	
2a	
3a	
4a	
5a	
1b	
2b	
3b	
4b	
5b	
1c	
2c	
3c	
4c	
5c	

Notes

Notes

Notes

Notes

Cambridge Checkpoint English
Stage 7